The Savvy Studio Owner

A Complete Guide to Setting Up and Running Your Own Recording Studio

Backbeat
Books

San Francisco

Published by Backbeat Books
600 Harrison Street, San Francisco, CA 94107
www.backbeatbooks.com
email: books@musicplayer.com

An imprint of the Music Player Network
Publishers of *Guitar Player*, *Bass Player*, *Keyboard*, and *EQ* magazines
United Entertainment Media, Inc.
A CMP Information Company

CMP
United Business Media

Distributed to the book trade in the US and Canada by
Publishers Group West, 1700 Fourth Street, Berkeley, CA 94710

Distributed to the music trade in the US and Canada by
Hal Leonard Publishing, P.O. Box 13819, Milwaukee, WI 53213

Text design by Maureen Forys, Happenstance Type-O-Rama
Composition by Maureen Forys, Happenstance Type-O-Rama
Cover design by Patrick Devine
Front cover photo by Andy Sotiriou/Getty Images

Library of Congress Cataloging-in-Publication Data

Shirley, John, 1969–
  The savvy studio owner : a complete guide to setting up and running your own recording studio / by John Shirley and Richard Strasser.
    p. cm.
  Includes index.
  ISBN-13: 978-0-87930-840-7
  ISBN-10: 0-87930-840-0 (alk. paper)
  1. Sound—Recording and reproducing. 2. Sound studios. 3. Music—Economic aspects. I. Strasser, Richard, 1966- II. Title.

TK7881.4.S48 2005
781.49'068—dc22

                              2005013343

Printed in the United States of America

05 06 07 08 09   5 4 3 2 1

Table of Contents

Introduction

Creating a hobby or recreational home recording studio is a rich and rewarding experience shared by thousands of people. At one point or another, many consider turning this hobby into a viable business that not only provides pleasure but also can be a lucrative source of income. Doing this is no easy matter. It takes a well-planned and well-executed approach. *The Savvy Studio Owner* was written to provide studio entrepreneurs with the tools and information needed to build a successful business.

Unlike other recording studio texts, *The Savvy Studio Owner* combines serious business planning with studio design and audio engineering. The result is a book written in clear and uncomplicated language that will help you understand the daily workings of a commercial recording studio.

Who Should Read This Book

This book is written for the entrepreneur with great drive, ambition, and a love of music. It will also provide valuable insight for others in the music business. Sound recording engineers, producers, musicians, managers, and even accountants and lawyers in the entertainment field can gain a lot from a more thorough understanding of this business and how it's run (or *should be* run).

Sound recording engineers will find the sections on business important in developing funding and keeping the recording studio afloat. It will also give them a better idea of how they fit into the overall scheme of the business, allowing them to work both more effectively and creatively. In smaller recording studios, the work of each individual has a great effect on the success of the whole.

Producers must be keenly aware of the business end of studio work, while also understanding the technical and theoretical elements of recording sessions and signal paths. In addition to artistic decisions, producers are often responsible for booking studios, hiring session musicians, and ensuring the artists are both comfortable and productive in their recording environment. In order to best deal with all of these organizational, financial, and personal tasks, producers need a thorough understanding of all aspects of the studio business.

Musicians should read this book to gain awareness of exactly what to expect from their studio and how to get the most out of it, both financially and artistically. In addition, this book can aid musicians in the smooth, cost-effective operation of home project studios.

Finally, accountants and lawyers who are retained by a recording studio will find this book helpful in dealing with such key areas as taxes, contractual relationships, litigation, and business structure.

How to Use This Book

This book was designed to guide a new recording studio owner through the process of starting, running, and expanding a recording studio. The chapters are organized around two thematic sections, with a detailed appendix that provides additional information and resources.

Part I: Setting Up Your Studio

The first section deals with the establishment of the recording studio, from planning and financing through acoustic design and equipment.

Part II: Running Your Studio

Readers who are already operating record studios may wish to begin here. Topics include marketing, legal issues, recording practices, employees, taxation, and expanding your business into areas such as video post-production, voice-overs, mastering, and duplication.

Appendix

This section includes important worksheets, Web resources, organizations, publications, and manufacturers that will allow you to keep in touch with an ever-changing industry.

Recent developments suggest that the future of the music business is taking place in small, independent recording studios. In a rapidly changing market, the recording and sale of music is moving away from large recording studios to the smaller, specialized studios that are creating new innovative styles (on a lower budget).

We hope that this book will answer many of your questions as you begin to record and create exciting and rewarding music in your own studio, and help you turn what you love doing into a profitable venture.

Part I
Setting Up Your Studio

1. Getting Started

After reading this chapter, you should be able to:
- Define the structure and function of a small business.
- Identify the traits that make an entrepreneur successful.
- Know the best time to start a recording studio.

Small businesses are considered to be the backbone of most thriving economies, including that of the United States. As a group, these businesses provide employment to a large part of the economy, pay taxes that keep state and local governments running, provide specialized goods and services, and develop the innovations that larger companies rely on and often absorb. With the advent of the Internet, the trend of developing large-scale companies with hundreds of employees has been reversed in favor of small, autonomous, exciting businesses.

Starting a new business can seem like a daunting task—a high-risk venture, both financially and personally. Many people think that those who are successful in turning a small business into a highly profitable enterprise have extraordinary powers, well beyond mortal souls. However, most successful entrepreneurs are ordinary people who possess certain traits that help them thrive as entrepreneurs. Let's look at seven key traits of successful entrepreneurs.

Self-Awareness
Successful entrepreneurs are aware of what they want to achieve and how to get it. They tend to know their limitations in trying to achieve too many things, and they handle the most important issues first before moving on to new tasks.

Motivation
Entrepreneurs are highly motivated people. They possess a drive that allows them to wake up every morning and focus on the job at hand or continue when the funds are scarce. They are genuinely interested in and excited about their services and products, while fully

understanding that the purpose of their business is to make a profit. Many recording studios fail because they lose sight of one or more of these primary concerns. To put it simply: If you don't love what you do, your product suffers. If you don't run your studio right, your profit suffers.

Knowledge
Knowledge is the key to getting things done and done right! It allows entrepreneurs to make shortcuts that keep others thinking for a long time.

Experience
Experience comes with trial and error. The most successful entrepreneurs rely on their experience to save time and money and to get things done. You can only gain experience by trying.

Persistence
Entrepreneurs never give up! They know that achieving their goals takes hardheaded determination. Many people have great ideas, but when they come across their first obstacle they often give up. An entrepreneur finds different ways of approaching the problems that all business owners face and learns from their errors.

Timing
Many people believe in luck. Entrepreneurs don't think luck exists but understand that timing is everything. They see when a product or service is required and take full advantage of that opportunity. If you don't possess that ability you will often see others take your idea and become successful before you do.

Thinking
The final trait of a successful entrepreneur is the ability to think, especially to think abstractly. If you constantly think through and plan for the future, your business will be safe no matter what develops.

Are You Ready to Be an Entrepreneur?

Now let's turn to six simple questions that every entrepreneur needs to answer before investing money or time in a project.

Who
Who will your customers be? For a studio owner, this question involves not only identifying potential customers but determining what style(s) of music you will specialize in. For example, you may love hip-hop but actually live in an area that has greater sales of country music. That may require you to either relocate or carve out a niche market in your area that has not been tapped into (we will cover that in the marketing section).

What

What are you going to do? Many recording studios today do much more than record music. They use their facilities for other music-related activities including rehearsals, music lessons, business recordings, and acoustic testing. The more services you have available for clients, the greater the chances of earning money.

Where

As noted above, the location of your studio can be extremely important in attracting customers and making money. Apart from geographical location, you should ask yourself if you intend to build your studio in your home or use a commercial space.

Why

This question is very easy to answer for most people who want to start a recording studio. First, you love the music you are recording and would like others to hear it too. Second, you want to make money doing something you enjoy. Finally, you have talent for recording music.

When

Timing can be the difference between success and total failure. Remember, there is never a better time than the present to begin planning your project.

How

How are you going to run your recording studio? Are you going to work alone, have partners, or form a company? Each of these options requires a different approach and has a different outcome.

Chapter Summary

1. Most successful entrepreneurs are ordinary people who possess certain traits, such as self-awareness, motivation, knowledge, experience, persistence, and timing.

2. Before you invest money or time in a project, you have to answer six basic questions: who your customers will be, what your business will offer, where you will be located, why you are starting the studio, when you will open your doors, and how you will run the studio.

2. Researching the Market

After reading this chapter, you should be able to:
- Research the music industry.
- Identify potential customers via market segmentation.
- Choose a location for the recording studio.
- Focus on specific services and markets.

Before you can open the doors of your studio, there are many preliminary steps you need to take, from researching the music industry to choosing a location, writing a business plan, and buying equipment. The size, function, and success of your studio will greatly depend on how you manage these factors.

It is important to remember that you create success through value, not by lowering costs. You can achieve this by developing a unique intellectual design and controlling your studio's resources.

Growth Stages of a Studio

As a new studio owner, it is important that you understand the stages in the life of a company. A normal studio will go through five stages from beginning to maturity. To reach the final stage, you need to understand these stages and the tasks associated with them.

Stage 1: Conception

At this stage you need to develop a concept of your recording studio. This includes an analysis of your potential customers and what products you want to deliver. You should also begin to think about your start-up costs. This factor will determine the size and scope of your recording studio.

Stage 2: Development

At this stage you move from a conceptual plan to an existing recording studio. It is essential that you generate enough money to stay in business, grow, and develop. Once the studio starts to become profitable you will be ready to move on to the next stage.

Stage 3: Stabilization

At this stage your studio has achieved economic stability, generating enough profit with a large clientele that you can expand and weather the bad times. You should begin to develop a marketing plan, which will be essential in progressing to the following stage and developing your recording studio's long-term goals.

Stage 4: Growth

At this stage your studio is financially healthy and ready to expand and hire staff. By delegating work to others, you can focus on the studio's creative direction rather than its financial survival.

Stage 5: Maturity

During this stage a recording studio often experiences rapid growth, thanks to its reputation in the music industry. Accompanying this growth is organizational complexity and increased need for finance, equipment, and labor. The owner must be able to handle the growth and be willing to give up power and control. Many studios also formulate an exit strategy at this stage, often through a buyout by a larger company or by obtaining capital for a future project with a separate business.

Researching the Music Industry

Research is an important part of developing any business. Large companies often use complex methods to obtain data that helps them develop and maintain the business in a highly competitive environment. Recording studio owners will also benefit by gathering primary and secondary research information.

Primary data is gathered to shed light on a specific problem through, for instance, focus groups, surveys, and interviews. Secondary data is information gathered through another source. Government agencies, such as the Census Bureau, and business associations are common sources of secondary data. A disadvantage of using secondary data is that it is often out of date, it may be too broad for your needs, or it may become irrelevant to your research when you need it most. However, secondary data has a decided advantage over primary data: gathering secondary data requires much less money and time.

The research you undertake will be used in designing your recording studio and attracting clients as well as securing financing. Researching the recording industry gives you an idea of how healthy the music sector is and what your likely profits will be. Like any industrial sector (e.g., mining, electronics, and airlines), the music industry fluctuates over time. During growth periods companies see increased profits, employees, and sales. The opposite is true during periods of recession; recording studios see lower profits, employee layoffs, and reduced sales. It is important to recognize whether the recording industry is going through a down period or up period and act accordingly.

For example, if the economy is doing poorly overall, record sales may be down. This means bands may not find work and not use your facilities to record new albums. However, if the economy is doing well and record sales are up, people may want to hear new groups, which will increase demand for your recording studio.

The majority of your data will come from secondary sources, and there are various resources you should investigate. For an overall view of the economy, the U.S. Census Bureau offers information on population trends, household income, and other aspects of the economy (www.census.gov). For information about the recording industry you should begin with *Billboard* magazine, a weekly journal that provides information and news about the music industry (www.billboard.com). For other important sources of secondary data, see the appendix.

Defining Your Market

Understanding who your customers will be is a very important step that affects numerous aspects of your recording studio. Doing this type of research will help you complete many tasks including: choosing an appropriate location, shaping your marketing strategy, finding a market, and defining the type of equipment you will need. Research into your potential clientele will save you money and time and sharpen many other facets of your recording studio.

The easiest way to select potential clients is by using a marketing method known as *market segmentation*. The primary objective of market segmentation is to group customers with similar wants, characteristics, and behaviors. This technique enables you to determine if a market is large enough to generate profit for your business.

Market segmentation traditionally is broken down into four main areas: geographic, demographic, psychographic, and behavioral segmentation. We will look at each of these four areas and how they impact your recording studio.

Geographic Segmentation

Geographic segmentation, as the title suggests, is based on the notion that consumers' needs and tastes vary by where they live. When applying this technique it is often best to begin in the

Common Demographic Segments

Age: Under 6, 6–11, 12–19, 20–34, 35–49, 50–64, 65+

Sex: Male, female

Family size: 1–2, 3–4, 5+

Family life cycle: Single; married, no children; married, youngest child under 6; married, youngest child over 6; other

Income: Under $2,500; $2,500–$10,000; $10,000–$20,000; $20,000–$50,000; $50,000 and over

Occupation: Professional and technical, retired, students, housewives, unemployed

Education: Grade school or less, some high school, high school graduate, college graduate

Race: White, black, Hispanic, Asian

macro level (country and state level) and continue to the micro level (county and city level). Three broad areas of geographical segmentation exist: urban, suburban, and rural. For the United States these areas can be broken down into four main regions: North East, South East, Central, and West. You may also break this grouping down further into smaller segments, giving you a more accurate definition of your intended market. These areas include: Pacific, Mountain, West North Central, West South Central, East North Central, East South Central, South Atlantic, and New England.

Most recording studios focus on a segmentation that is based on city size. This segmentation, based on population numbers and the potential growth of population, gives you an idea of the number of potential customers in a specific city and its surrounding suburbs. The main source of information for geographic segmentation in the U.S. is the Census Bureau.

Demographic Segmentation

Demographic segmentation involves dividing a market into groups based on variables such as age, sex, family size, family life cycle, income, etc. It is the most widely used of the segmenting techniques since the results can be easily defined and measured. Many media outlets use demographic segmentation to reach their intended market, and it is especially important for advertising.

Psychographic Segmentation

Psychographic segmentation is based on consumers' psychological makeup, including their social roles, personality, and lifestyles. Psychographic marketing deals with how consumers approach products and how they behave with respect to a certain product. For example, people within a certain social group will purchase products to keep their status within the group. Psychographic segmentation also deals with personality types such as compulsive, gregarious, and ambitious, to mention a few.

Behavioral

The final way to segment a market is based on the benefits sought from a studio's products. Behavioral segmentation considers if people are nonusers, potential users, or regular users; if they have particular loyalty to a product; and if they have any particular attitude to a product (e.g., enthusiastic, positive, indifferent, negative, or hostile).

Expanding Your Services

When considering possible customers and markets, new studio owners often make the mistake of creating too narrow an initial business plan, based on their enthusiasm for a particular style of music. For example, while creating a studio dedicated to the art and careers of local metal bands may seem like a noble idea at first, such overspecialization may contribute to the failure of a studio.

Defining a more diverse base of services, and therefore clientele, is not only a sound business approach but can also lead to a more rewarding experience in the studio. Both personal interest and creative inspiration benefit from exposure to new experiences. Fortunately, the basic equipment and skills needed to open and operate a studio are the same for numerous musical genres as well as many other audio-related tasks.

The following is a breakdown of some possible areas to consider.

Music Groups/Solo Artists

There are several ways that clients can go about booking studio time. Record labels, both small independents and the majors, often have one or more studios they recommend for their artists. It is a good strategy to nurture this kind of relationship with local labels. Similarly, record producers (hired by a label or the artists themselves) often recommend or request studios in which they've worked and found success. Get cozy with producers and offer them financial incentives to book with your studio (such as price breaks for larger blocks of time or multiple bands). You might even offer free studio time for the personal projects that many producers have. Finally, many artists book studio time directly. This is especially true when they are recording demos but can also be the case if they are already signed to a label.

An interesting subcategory of solo artists is the vocalist doing covers of prerecorded music. Often these people are local entertainers assembling a demo CD to help them book gigs, singers looking to impress an A&R person with their talent, or amateurs making a recording for fun to give to family and friends. In some cases, these clients look for the studio to supply an instrumental version of a popular song they wish to sing over. While it is financially impractical for a small studio to buy an extensive library of songs for this purpose, having a few karaoke CDs around can be handy. You can meet client requests for particular songs, made ahead of time, by ordering appropriate materials quickly online.

Remixes & Club Music

Producers of remixes and music designed specifically for clubs are now fairly common and represent an all-too-often ignored or misunderstood part of a recording studio's potential market. This area has become quite lucrative in the last decade. In order to attract and service these clients, a studio needs to be equipped with stylistically appropriate synthesizers, drum machines, and samplers as well as the MIDI interfaces and sequencers to control them.

Furthermore, since many of these projects begin in a home studio, engineers should possess a thorough knowledge of audio formats as well as the technical ability to convert from one to another. Smaller studios may require a network of subcontractors or the occasional rental of extra equipment, because it is often impractical to purchase platforms in all of the major formats. Fortunately, there are also some inexpensive computer interfaces on the market that can aid in the transfer of audio from one format to another (at this writing, the most notable is the 2408mk3 from Mark of the Unicorn).

Full compatibility requires knowledge of topics to be discussed later in this book: ADAT, Lightpipe, USB, Firewire (IEEE-1394), Tascam DA-38/88/78, T-DIF, OMF, SCSI, MIDI, S/PDIF, AES/EBU, and Macintosh vs. PC file formats.

Mastering & Duplication Services

Once a final mix of a recording is made, the next steps are mastering and duplication. Offering these services not only expands your client base but exposes the studio to musicians who may have used another facility for their current recording, but may well record the next project in your studio once they have experienced your good work in the mastering arena.

Mastering is the act of creating a final version that is ready for, and will sound the best on, its final delivery format. Professional quality compression, limiting, EQ, noise reduction, monitoring, dither, CD burning, and sample rate conversion are the basic tools needed, and these are often already a part of a well-designed studio. Mastering requires a good ear for sonic balance, and experience with how audio translates among various playback and delivery systems.

Duplication services describes a host of services including the creation, preparation, duplication, and insertion of artwork in (or on) a CD, cassette, DVD, vinyl record, or any other audio/video delivery format. Duplication services also include mastering, as well as the actual duplication/fabrication of the final media product. Many providers of these services perform only one (and sometimes none) of these steps themselves, preferring to organize the process while subcontracting the individual tasks.

Location Recording

Many recording opportunities occur outside the confines of the recording studio. Church groups, schools, performing ensembles, and gigging bands often make location recordings. Another possibility is working with one of the many companies that compile sample libraries.

If a studio is equipped with a portable recording device (such as a DAT, ADAT, DA-38/88/78, laptop, or other proprietary portable recorder) and movable microphone preamplifiers, then it has the basics required for this sort of work. All of the cabling, stands, condenser microphones, and editing software/hardware needed are already a part of any professional studio.

Voice-overs, Music Beds & Sound Design

Local radio stations sometimes hire studios to do work they cannot do in house for lack of equipment, space, personnel, or time. Projects could include public service and promotional announcements, ads, sound effects for DJs, and sound montages.

Advertising agencies and multimedia companies use studios to serve a variety of audio needs. These include editing, format conversion, voice-overs, music beds, and sound effects as well as mastering and post-production tasks. Similarly, Web design companies and creators of computer games often need a steady supply of clean voice-over recordings, music beds, and sound effects. Large companies also create specialized recordings for announcements, voice-mail systems, on-hold messages, and internal training and promotional purposes.

Finally, there's a steady need for studios to record voice-overs for audio books based on textbooks, novels, manuals, and workbooks. Contact the publishers of either the audio versions or the original texts to track down who may hire studios for this work.

Extra equipment needed for these tasks might include sample libraries (available online, but often with audible artifacts or restricted frequency content), synthesizers, drum machines, and samplers.

Post-Production

Many local videographers and video-editing facilities serve local businesses in the creation of television commercials, promotional videos, and Web-based advertisements, as well as wedding and other personal videos. While they have the capability of recording and editing audio, the quality is often poor due to a lack of knowledge or the natural tendency to overfocus on the video portion of a project. In addition, lower-quality microphones, preamps, cabling, and effects are used. These service providers are often aware of, and frustrated by, these shortcomings. Many of them are relieved to leave the technical aspects of the final audio editing and mixdown to someone else, whose help will allow them to deliver a much higher-quality final product. In this capacity, the studio acts as a subcontractor.

Additional equipment such as video decks (now usually S-VHS and/or DV-Pro), SMPTE time-code readers, and editing software, which can slave to SMPTE or PC video, is sometimes required for this type of work.

Rental of Studio Space

One way to supplement the income of a studio still building a client base, or one that is trying to maximize income during cyclical slow periods, is to rent studio rooms for rehearsals or musical instrument lessons. Both functions serve not only to generate income but also as a sort of advertising, exposing more musicians (a.k.a. prospective clients) to the studio. Many will come back to record in the future.

Retail Sales

Limited retail sales of products such as sheet music, books, strings, tuners, capos, slides, and cables can add studio income while offering a further service and convenience to local musicians. Inexpensive instruments such as harmonica, jaw harp, kazoo, recorder, fife, and shakers can be tempting impulse purchases to bands spending time recording and looking to add some interesting sounds to their project.

A studio can earn further supplemental income by offering CDs of music recorded at the studio, taken on a consignment basis from the band, label, or distributor.

Finally, don't forget that people stuck in the studio may need a handy supply of sodas and snacks.

Choosing a Location

After researching your potential clientele and the economic conditions in which your studio will operate, the next step is choosing your recording studio's location. The location can make the difference between a studio's success or failure. Planning ahead before you move is extremely important, as you can expect to remain in an area for some time. Remember, moving is expensive and your current customers may not follow you to a new location.

Let's look at some important factors that influence your choice of a location for your recording studio.

Type of Business

There are three types of businesses in today's market: retail, production, and service businesses. Each type has an influence on the location of a store.

Retail businesses are concerned with drawing people into the store to make a purchase. Therefore, high visibility and access are important factors in choosing a location.

Production companies convert raw materials into products. They sell these products to an intermediary (distributor) who passes them on to the customer. Therefore, keeping costs down is more important in choosing a location than trying to attract customers to the store.

A service-based business—such as a recording studio—has characteristics of a retailer and producer. It must be centrally located to attract customers, while being mindful of costs for the services offered.

Many service businesses start and operate out of the owner's home. This arrangement is often a good solution if you don't have enough money to buy or lease commercial space. Keeping your recording studio at home also has the advantage of lowering your costs and tax levels.

However, locating your studio in an area with other businesses can increase visibility and help you expand your clientele.

Government Regulations & Taxes

Government regulations and taxes are important factors in choosing a location. Numerous government regulations affect the operation of businesses in a particular area (details will be covered in a later chapter). Federal, state, and local governments levy a variety of taxes including personal, corporate, sales, and property taxes. Be sure to look at the tax rate your recording studio will pay in a potential location.

Appearance

The outward appearance of your studio conveys a sense of professionalism to potential clients. It is important that your signage corresponds to local regulations and laws. If you are using a commercial space, the rules vary according to your lease and location. Remember that the signage used in a strip mall needs to be large enough to attract road traffic.

Shipping & Loading Space

Be sure to consider shipping and loading space in choosing your location. If you are located in a residential neighborhood, a few small deliveries will not disturb the peace of your fellow residences. However, if you deliver larger units or if visiting groups bring in large instruments and equipment, you may need to alter your location plans. Many local governments have strict laws regarding the use of residential zones for business. It is highly recommended that you check with your local government on what is allowed before starting a business at home.

Utilities

All business must deal with utilities, including electricity, water, telephone, and heating. On the audio side of things, electricity is the utility of primary concern. Many studio audio devices are quite sensitive to problems caused by poor electrical service. They can be damaged and/or their performance can be compromised. Potential problems include computer crashes, loss of data, equipment power supply burnouts, audio hum or buzz, inconsistent system performance, and reduction of signal-to-noise ratio.

There are hardware solutions capable of stabilizing and purifying the incoming electrical signal, but the more thorough solutions are often very expensive and cannot always be relied upon completely. It is certainly best to start with good service.

A licensed electrician can help determine if a location meets these necessary criteria:

- Proper grounding.

- Steady, constant voltage between 115 and 120 volts.

- Few brownouts.

- Limited spikes and line noise.

- All wiring and breakers appropriate for 20-amp circuits.

When considering a location you should also take note of any dimmers or fluorescent bulbs. They will have to be removed so they won't cause unwanted noise in the audio path. Externally, look and listen for any transformers nearby. If they are too close, they can also compromise audio quality by adding hum.

Of course, the studio's electrical system also needs to meet fundamental standards for safety. One sure sign that there are severe, possibly hazardous electrical problems is the smell of ozone near the breaker box, outlets, switches, or other appliances. Most people are familiar with this "electrical smell," which is often experienced with old kitchen appliances, motors on toys (especially electric cars and trains), old amplifiers, and fussy switches or dimmers. If the specific problem is not found and fixed, you should not accept the location for your studio. Also beware any other olfactory signals for electrical issues such as the scent of hot/melting plastic or rubber, or any hint of something burning.

Transportation

Transportation links are important in attracting customers. Access to major highways is important, so that regional traffic can easily reach you. Likewise, public transportation is an important factor in attracting people without their own means of transportation. This group includes students, who could be the majority of your potential customer base.

Noise

There are two important factors to consider when looking at noise issues in a studio location. The first is the amount of noise that is generally experienced inside the space during the course of the day. This includes both inside noise (from ducts, radiators, lighting, plumbing, etc.) and outside noise (traffic, airplanes, trains, neighbors' stereos, firing ranges, church bells, schools, other businesses). In both cases you need to know what the average background noise level is as well as what sorts of momentary peaks to expect.

Of course, the studio space can be acoustically treated and modified to minimize these problems, but once again it is best to start with something good and make it better rather than trying to fix up something lousy. The latter is a very expensive and risky proposition.

The level of ambient noise should be determined throughout the day and under all normal, expected working conditions. For example, you should measure noise when it's raining, when any neighbors or adjoining businesses are going about their routines, and when the heat and/or air-conditioning are turned on.

With experience, you can partially determine the acceptability of some of these factors by ear. To get the most accurate and complete picture, however, you should make more scientific and accurate measurements. If the studio budget allows, you can hire an acoustician to collect the appropriate data and give advice on the suitability of a location. Relatively inexpensive noise-measuring devices are also available that can be used as long as you are careful to follow all instructions and have a thorough understanding of the device's function. Read the manual carefully.

Measurements will be taken in units of dB(SPL), short for decibels of sound pressure level. In addition, a device may offer peak (sometimes called fast) and RMS (slow) options. Peak measurements are most sensitive to instantaneous sound, while RMS settings generate more of an average level reading over time. Finally, there are frequency weighting schemes as well. You should use both A and C weightings when taking measurements.

The A-weighted measurements more accurately represent how the human ear would perceive the relative levels of ambient sound across the frequency spectrum. Most notably, the ear is less sensitive to low-frequency energy.

C-weighted measurements, on the other hand, more closely represent the actual sound energy across the frequency spectra, even the low end. It is important to take this type of reading as well since low-frequency sounds, which may go unnoticed by the listener, can cause distortion or a lack of clarity in a recording. With the increasing use of subwoofers, more and more systems are now equipped to reproduce and accentuate the lower octaves. Bass problems that went unnoticed in the studio can be heard glaringly when played back on a home theater system.

A room without any specialized studio acoustic treatments should measure a maximum of 35 to 42dB(SPL), either A or C weighted. A range of 30 to 35dB(SPL) would be a better start. Ideally, these ranges would be achieved even with the heating or air-conditioning running. Once the space is treated, these ranges should come down to the 1 to 20dB(SPL) range, especially for the isolation areas.

Security

A studio is a rather high-visibility business with many small but valuable assets. You must therefore pay attention to finding a relatively secure location, recording all equipment serial numbers and prices, locking up any microphones or other expensive items when not in use, and securing all other equipment to desks or racks so that they cannot be easily removed. Be sure that everything is fully insured as well.

Zoning Laws

Most cities in the United States have zoning ordinances that control the use of areas for residential single- and two-family homes, apartments, and commercial usage. However, zoning laws can be vague about what precisely is considered residential and whether it can be used for a home-based business.

Many cities require that people use their homes for "home occupation." Using your home for professional purposes depends on several factors including: the amount of car and truck traffic, usage of outside signs, on-street parking, the number of employees, and the percentage of floor space devoted to the business in comparison to the amount used for living. Enforcement of zoning laws also varies widely. Much of the government's action depends on residents enforcing the law and notifying the authorities. With mounting pressure from residents, local municipalities may order a cease-and-desist letter, followed by a misdemeanor prosecution or a civil lawsuit leading to fines or, in extreme cases, jail time for violations of local zoning laws.

It is imperative to research local zoning laws and enforcement of those laws before starting your studio from home. When you file your local business license or tax permit, local officials may question you on the validity of your operations. It is in your best interest to deal with zoning issues before you buy a home for the purposes of a business or commence your recording studio.

The best way to avoid problems is to be a good neighbor. Keep traffic levels down, be sensitive about sound pollution, and keep signage to respectable levels.

Commercial vs. Home Locations

Let's take a closer look at the pros and cons of renting a commercial space and setting up a studio in your home.

Commercial Locations

Setting up your recording studio in a commercial space has several advantages over a home-based recording studio, including appearance, complementary businesses, shipping and loading facilities, and access.

Your appearance says a lot about your company. A company's visibility includes external advertising, such as signage to attract potential customers. Commercial spaces allow companies to use signage on the exterior of the building as well as near roads to attract passers-by.

An industrial zone gives you the opportunity to be close to other companies that offer auxiliary products for your company. For example, you could be in an industrial zone that is located close to compact disc manufacturing and printing offices. You could offer your customers the opportunity to record and press albums without traveling to several areas to complete the work.

An industrial zone also allows your studio to have full access to shipping and loading facilities. Many local ordinances do not allow trucks of a certain tonnage to operate within residential areas. You may also face clashes with neighbors if trucks are blocking access to residences. Often industrial zones have good access to major travel routes, allowing easy access for your customers and deliveries.

A very important issue to consider in using commercial sites is leasing. It is important that you balance the cost of renting against the potential for profit. A savings of several hundred dollars in rent may result in thousands of dollars lost in sales if your customers cannot find you. You should also consider the amount of capital you have to sign a lease or purchase the property. If you constantly fall short of the amounts needed, a real estate agent may not show you properties in the future. Obtaining the funding to lease a commercial space is covered in a later chapter.

Home-Based Business

A home location may be perfect for a person beginning a recording studio on a tight budget. Not only can you use the facilities to establish a small business, but you can also live in the space. Getting on well with people around you will help keep the peace and avoid litigation, so remember these points:

- Make sure your house number is clearly marked so that clients will not go to the wrong house.

- Have any deliveries by large trucks, which are often noisy and block the street, come at a time that is appropriate for your neighbors. You could also invest in storage away from your house and purchase a post office box to reduce deliveries to your home.

- Be aware of the time when recording. You may be inspired to record a loud heavy metal band at one in the morning, but your neighbors may not share your enthusiasm.

- Be mindful of zoning laws with regard to home-based businesses.

Chapter Summary

1. Before opening a recording studio, use both primary and secondary data to understand the current state of the industry and the likelihood of success.

2. Use market segmentation to identify potential clientele. This means knowing consumers' needs, attitudes, and buying behavior by dividing a market into homogenous groups. The four most common factors used to identify segments are demographics, geography, psychographics, and behavior.

3. Understand the various income streams and avenues of specialization for a studio.

4. Choose a location that best suits your studio, taking into account external factors such as government regulations and taxes, shipping, utilities, and transportation needs.

5. Recognize the difference between commercial and residential zoning and how it affects a home-based business.

3. Business Structure

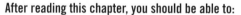

After reading this chapter, you should be able to:

- Understand the various business entities in existence.
- Know what the legal requirements are for a sole proprietorship.
- Define the two types of partnerships.
- Complete the proper documentation for incorporation.

Now that you have researched the business environment, studied your potential client base, and found a suitable location for your recording studio, it is time to shape your recording studio's business structure. All businesses must have a legal structure, correct business licenses, and a legally trademarked name.

Your choice of business structure is influenced by many factors, including:

- Your liability needs. What legal protection will you need?

- Capital. How much money do you have, or how much will you be able to obtain?

- Size. How big do you want your recording studio to be?

- Goals. What are your short- and long-term goals for the studio?

- Federal, state, and local regulations. What legal requirements do you have to meet for licenses, taxes, etc.?

Legal Structures

There are three basic types of business structure in existence today: sole proprietorship, partnership, and corporation. Each business structure has its own characteristic legal status, size, tax considerations, funding, and internal structure, and each has inherent advantages and disadvantages. The choice of a particular form is in no way set in stone. Often a business evolves from a sole proprietorship to a partnership and finally becomes a corporation.

Sole Proprietorship

A sole proprietorship is a business owned by one person. It is the oldest and most common form of business structure, as well as the least expensive to start. Many small business owners prefer a proprietorship not only because of the simplicity of start-up, but because of the relative freedom of control, operation, and dissolution. Another advantage of a sole proprietorship is that you do not have to publish an annual report, as you do with a corporation. This allows you to keep many of your business details and goals secret. Finally, a sole proprietorship has tax advantages over other forms of business. Sole proprietorships pay tax at the lower personal income tax rate rather than the higher corporate rate. (See the later section on taxes.)

No formal documentation is required to start a studio as a sole proprietorship. If you have employees or have a studio that must comply with government regulation, such as by paying sales tax, you will need to follow formal guidelines. You may use your own name for your studio title, as long as another company does not use it. Alternatively, you may file for the use of a fictitious name for your recording studio. This requires you to file a doing-business-as certificate or fictitious-name statement with your local chamber of commerce. It is also a good idea to obtain a trademark to protect your assets. (See chapter 12 for more information on trademark applications.)

There are some disadvantages of operating a sole proprietorship. New businesses in general require large amounts of capital to purchase equipment, lease facilities, pay employees, etc. Unless you have vast personal assets, it is often difficult to obtain funding to start your recording studio. Lenders often see a recording studio operated by one person as a risk, compared to a studio run by a group of people with greater equity. For this reason, sole proprietors may find it difficult to secure a bank loan to buy new equipment. The sole proprietor of a studio is also personally responsible for all of the company's debts. That includes your personal assets, which may be seized to pay off creditors, even if the debt was not your fault. Finally, because the business and the owner are legally the same, at the death of the owner a recording studio must dissolve. That requires anyone who has a vested interest in the company to reform the studio's business structure, going through the same process of filing forms, obtaining licenses, etc.

General Partnership

A partnership is a voluntary business relationship between two or more persons. A partnership is similar in many respects to a sole proprietorship, but it is often more difficult to form, operate, and terminate. The advantages of a partnership over a sole proprietorship include the ability to obtain capital more easily, the collective expertise of many members, and the longer legal life span of the studio.

Within the umbrella term of partnership, there are two divisions: general and limited. In a general partnership the public knows all partners, and each partner assumes the responsibility of liability for the studio. In a limited partnership there are one or more general partners and several limited partners, whom the general public may or may not know. These limited partners often have no role in the operation and management of the business;

they give that responsibility to the general partners and are only liable for the amount of capital they contributed to the studio. The details of each partner's responsibilities, rights, and duties are expressed in the articles of copartnership. This document is essential, as it clearly outlines the roles and function of each partner. All profits and losses are distributed to the partners and are taxed at personal tax rates.

Unlike a sole proprietorship, a partnership has an unlimited life span. A business may continue as long as it wishes, without the need to reassign at the death of a partner. In addition, each partner is protected from liability in the articles of copartnership.

A fundamental drawback to a partnership is the potential for interpersonal difficulties. These could occur with unproductive members, disagreements between members, and conflicts that may arise when one partner wishes to leave the studio. In some cases a partner who leaves the recording studio may take important plans and clients to a rival studio.

A partnership by name is an agreement between several members that must be in writing or implied by law. The partnership agreement does not require filing with a government agency, but there are some important documents needed by government agencies. Some states require registration to identify the studio and its partners. As with a sole proprietorship, general partnerships are required to obtain a vendor's or sales tax license in the appropriate state. Similarly, in many states a partnership must file a fictitious-name registration if it uses a name other than the names of the partners. Additionally, the IRS requires the partnership to file for an employer identification number (EIN) for withholding taxes.

Limited Liability Partnership

A recent development has been the creation of the limited liability partnership (LLP). Similar in some respects to a partnership, an LLP limits the members of the partnership to two or more individuals in the same profession. Furthermore, the partnership requires members to make decisions by majority vote on the basis of their percentage of ownership. Liability in an LLP is restricted to individual members. Partners in a LLP must file a certificate of limited liability partnership with the secretary of state. Each state requires certain materials, but generally the certificate should contain the name of the business, the partners involved, and the term of the LLP.

Strategic Partnership

Specific projects often require businesses to form short-term relationships with other companies. These strategic partnerships have a comparative advantage over traditional partnerships and corporations in that the combined resources of the partnering organizations can be greater than those of a traditional business. These types of structures can reduce business expenses and risk in an economic downturn.

A joint venture is a cooperative partnership in which organizations share investments, costs, and profits in developing products. Created for a short period of time, these partnerships often dissolve after the completion of a particular task. The advantage of such an arrangement is that studios can join for a short period of time without long-term obligations, use each studio's specialized skills, and dissolve the partnership after the project is completed. Joint ventures are formed by either an oral or written agreement that covers areas such as capital contribution, control, and the distribution of profits and losses. If you use a fictitious name for the joint venture, you need to file a certificate with the secretary of state. If your joint venture hires employees, it must follow federal and state laws.

Liability in a joint venture is also similar to a general partnership, with liability based on the partner's business entity. Therefore, if one partner is a corporation, its individual partners are not liable. However, if the other partner is a sole proprietorship, the individual is responsible for any liabilities.

Cooperatives occur when several companies with common goals work collectively to obtain greater bargaining power, pool resources, and compete against larger companies, as witnessed in the agricultural sector. In a cooperative, each member receives an equal portion of the profits.

Corporation

Corporations or C corporations are legal entities in which the obligations and legal status exist independently of the owners. In this structure, shareholders are responsible for hiring and firing management, but are not responsible for the legal dealings of the corporation. Individuals or other companies can purchase shares, also known as stock, of the corporation. The combination of unlimited life span and the ability to obtain capital give corporations the potential for growth not often seen in sole proprietorships or partnerships. If an owner wishes to maintain control of the corporation, he or she can own it privately and trade the stock on the open market, forming a private corporation.

The main advantage of corporations is their ability to attract money, resources, and people to achieve specific goals. Furthermore, corporations have the advantage of liquidity: the ability to convert stock into cash, something that is difficult to do in a sole proprietorship or partnership. There are two types of stock: preferred stock and common stock. Upon liquidation of a corporation, preferred stockholders receive any assets before common stockholders. They receive a fixed rate of return on their investments. For example, the owner of 5 percent preferred stock receives dividends based on the fixed rate of return of 5 percent. As with liquidation, preferred stockholders receive their dividends (part of a company's net earnings paid to stockholders) before common stockholders.

A major disadvantage of a corporation is the cost and time needed to incorporate. State rules on incorporation vary greatly, and it is prudent to consult with a lawyer and accountant before beginning the process. Individual stockholders are also required to pay income tax on dividends, so a corporation in effect pays tax twice—unlike proprietorships and partnerships, which only pay once. Another disadvantage of incorporation is public disclosure of business activities via an annual report. This gives competitors an opportunity to investigate the corporation in order to gain an advantage. Public disclosure may also provide enough information for a rival corporation to plan a takeover.

Corporate owners file articles of incorporation with the secretary of state in the state in which it wants to be incorporated. Legal considerations often influence the choice of state for incorporation. For example, many companies incorporate in Delaware, which has a reputation for handling shareholder or control issues quickly. Generally, articles of incorporation describe the purpose and structure of the company. The information required for incorporation includes:

- Name of the corporation. This must be an original name, for trademark reasons.

- Duration of the corporation. Most corporations elect to be perpetual.

- Purpose of the organization.

- Name of each director.

- Capital stock structure, including the class (preferred or common), quantity, and rights of the stock (voting or nonvoting), and preemptive rights (stock ownership rights such as first refusal of a stockholder to purchase new shares).

- Name and address of each incorporator.

- Name of the statutory agent or registered agent.

In many states a corporation is also required to file corporate bylaws. This is a written statement of the day-to-day management of the corporation, including meeting procedures, description of the officer's functions and duties, etc.

Limited Liability Company

A limited liability company (LLC) offers the best traits of a partnership and a corporation. In an LLC, an owner has limited liability protection, as in a corporation. Unlike with a corporation, owners (rather than the stockholders) receive profits. Therefore, an LLC is only taxed once.

LLC formation, like corporations, requires the filing of articles of organization with the secretary of state in the state of incorporation. Requirements for the articles of organization include:

- Name and address of the LLC.

- Name and address of the registered agent.

- The purpose of the LLC.

- The initial contribution of each member.

- Duration of the LLC.

As with corporation bylaws, an operating agreement functions as a guide to the management of an LLC. At the core of this agreement is an arrangement among the members, including the initial capital contribution, members' voting rights, authority of the members, membership transfer, and members' duties and rights at dissolution.

S Corporation

The S corporation or subchapter S corporation is a specialized corporate structure that allows for limited stockholders, who are taxed at personal income tax rates. To obtain the payments the shareholders must file form 2553 with the IRS. Furthermore, stockholders can only be individuals, estates, or personal trusts. Other companies cannot invest in the company, which eliminates the possibility of a hostile takeover. In 1996 the Small Business Job Protection Act increased the maximum number of shareholders to 75 from the previous limit of 35. This increased the potential capital that S corporations can obtain in the market. Unlike regular corporations, S corporations file one class of stock. After fulfilling the requirements for C incorporation, you may elect S corporation status for federal income tax purposes.

Chapter Summary

1. Sole proprietorships are the easiest business entities to form. As a sole proprietor, you are taxed at the individual rate and do not file incorporation papers or an annual report. You will be personally liable for all debts incurred by you or your staff. A sole proprietorship dissolves at the death of the owner.

2. Partnerships are divided into two categories: general and limited. General partnerships consist of members known to the public. Limited partnerships have limited partners, who are not publicly recognized, and general partners, who operate the business on a daily basis. Each partner is liable for any debt in the company, but the partnership can last indefinitely.

3. Strategic partnerships are formed for specific tasks. Joint ventures are specialized partnerships between companies, often formed for a short period to complete a specific task. Cooperatives occur when several companies with common goals work collectively.

4. Corporations are legal entities in which the obligations exist independently of the owners. This power is transferred to shareholders, who can elect and fire a corporation's management. Corporations are double taxed and operate in perpetuity.

5. A limited liability company (LLC) offers the benefits of a partnership (single taxation) and a corporation (limited liability). S corporations are specialized entities with a limit on the number of shareholders who are taxed at personal income rates.

4. Financial Planning

After reading this chapter you should be able to:
- Understand the principles of financial management of a recording studio.
- Prepare a personal financial history.
- Identify important documents and terms associated with financial planning.
- Create an income statement, cash flow statement, balance sheet, and break-even analysis.
- Prepare a business plan for your studio.
- Understand the importance of accountants and lawyers in achieving your financial goals.

For a recording studio owner, the purpose of financial planning is to formulate a credible and comprehensive set of projections for the studio's financial performance. These projections indicate a studio's financial stature to investors, partners, and anyone wishing to conduct business with the studio. Unlike other sections of a business plan, the financial plan deals with the bottom line (or net income) of your studio.

Before you open your studio, you must set up a record-keeping system that gives you information about sales, receipts, disbursements, and any stock you carry. Don't wait until after you are in business to set up this system—it may be too late. Today there are several simple-to-use spreadsheet programs that allow you to keep accurate records of your finances.

If you are starting a new studio, your financial documents are presumptions, since your studio has no financial history. It is therefore imperative to put your projections into proper perspective by considering more than one financial scenario, ranging from conservative estimates to projections based on the studio's full potential. These financial scenarios should also conform to details presented in other sections of the business plan.

As a new recording studio owner you should look to your own finances to see if you are able to finance your operation by yourself. In this chapter you'll find tools for measuring your personal finances and your potential costs. Corresponding worksheets are supplied in the appendix.

Basic Financial Statements

There are several important financial statements that you need to operate your studio. Each statement has a specific purpose and should be completed on a daily, weekly, monthly, and quarterly basis. These documents are important because they will not only show you how well your studio is doing, but help you borrow money from banks and other lending institutions. Establishing specific goals and achieving them instills trust in your banker and helps you to grow in the future.

There are four documents you will need to prepare to obtain financial backing.

Income Statement
Income statements reflect quarterly performance of the studio for a specific period of time. Typically they cover a five-year period, with the first three years expressed annually and the most recent two years expressed quarterly or annually.

Cash Flow Statement
A cash flow statement shows how much money was made and where it went. This statement gives a good picture of how a company can pay its short-term debts. A cash flow statement for a new studio would show the first two years of operation.

Balance Sheet
A balance sheet reflects the financial position of the company at a particular period, typically at the end of a financial period. End-of-year balance sheets should be prepared.

Break-Even Analysis
A break-even analysis expresses the break-even point for your studio, where your studio has balanced all costs and expenses against sales. This is represented as point zero. After this point your studio will begin to generate a profit.

Key Terms

Before we begin to construct these financial statements we need to define several important terms.

Assets
Assets are things a studio can use to generate income. They can be divided into fixed assets, which are long-term investments, and current assets, which include cash or items that have high liquidity (meaning they can easily be converted into cash). It is important that you take stock of your assets, as they will be used in your balance sheet and other statements.

Liabilities
Liabilities or expenses are claims against the studio's assets. They could take the form of money that the studio owes to suppliers, for short- or long-term loans, and for

miscellaneous services (such as electricity, telephone, etc.). Current liabilities are obligations that are due within a period of one year. Long-term liabilities are obligations that are due beyond a period of one year. Liabilities are often listed in the order in which they are due.

As a new studio owner, the most important liabilities you face are start-up costs. Start-up costs for a studio include fixtures and equipment, starting inventory, decorating and remodeling, installation of equipment, deposits for utilities, legal and professional fees, licenses and permits, advertising, and operating cash.

These start-up costs can be represented as two types of expenses: controllable and fixed expenses. Controllable expenses include supplies, services, and items purchased for use in the studio. These include regular maintenance and repair of equipment, advertising costs, and the use of outside professional services, such as accounting and legal services. Fixed expenses are those that do not change regardless of the number of units produced. You can estimate your start-up costs using the worksheet supplied in the appendix.

Owner's Equity

Owner's equity is the amount of money that belongs to the owners after all the obligations to creditors have been met. It is measured by taking assets minus liabilities. If you are a sole proprietorship, you just list your owner's equity under your name. If your studio is structured as a partnership, list each partner's share. Finally, if your studio is set up as a corporation, you need to list the amount of stock owned by each shareholder. Together with liabilities and assets, owner's equity is part of the basic accounting equation:

Assets = liabilities + owner's equity

Income Statement

An income statement (also known as a profit and loss statement) allows a studio owner to develop a preview of the amount of income generated each month and for the business year. For a new studio the statement is structured around predictions of monthly sales, costs, and expenses. These predictions can serve as goals for controlling business operations and expenses. As an indicator of financial performance, the income statement is read by creditors such as banks or other financial lending companies. It is important that the income statement indicates the studio's ability to pay the principle of a loan on a monthly basis.

An income statement expresses two important categories: revenues (net sales) and expenses (cost of sales, operating expenses, and taxes).

Total Net Sales

The first step in creating the income statement is estimating the total sales you will make during a month at specific prices after costs have been accounted for. This figure will form the basis of your net sales figure. It will also help you determine your pricing policy.

Cost of Sales

Cost of sales is a measurement of how much it costs your studio to sell its services. These costs have an effect on the total net sales for the studio, especially where inventory is involved. When estimating inventory costs, include the cost of transportation and direct labor in your calculations.

Gross Profit

To determine your gross profit, subtract the total costs of sales from the total net sales. This figure is what you intend to make before expenses and taxes. You need to look at your liabilities from the last section to calculate your expenses.

Operating Expenses

After establishing your gross profit you need to calculate your operating expenses. The operating expenses are all the costs that are not included under cost of goods sold. These include:

- Salary expenses (if you have employees), including overtime.
- Payroll expenses including health insurance, unemployment insurance, and Social Security.
- Repairs and maintenance of equipment.
- Utilities.
- Advertising and sales promotion.
- Depreciation of your capital assets.
- Rent.
- Licenses and permit fees.

Some income statements include all expenses under a general expense category. They combine general expenses (utilities, maintenance), property tax, and administrative expenses (salaries) into a single amount for selling, general, and administrative expenses (often abbreviated as SG&A expenses).

Income from Operations

Income from operations is a measurement of how much your studio made from its operations. In other words, this is the income received from recording.

Other Income

The income statement also includes income derived from bank and other financial organization loans. This is expressed as interest income, but you need to include the expense or loss you have incurred by purchasing this interest (losses are shown in parentheses).

Taxes

To develop your income statement you also need to determine your taxes. A detailed study of taxes is found in the next chapter. The taxes used in your income statement include inventory tax (the tax paid for your inventory), sales taxes (if you have them in your state), and any real estate taxes owed. After these calculations, you will have a figure that represents your net profit/loss after taxes.

Operating expenses and income taxes are deducted from the gross profit to establish the studio's net income or loss for the period.

Cash Flow Statement

A cash flow projection allows you to see if you are bringing in enough money each month to pay your bills and keep your studio operating at its maximum. Businesses go through cycles, and preparing a cash flow statement helps you prepare for the financial peaks and valleys. To prepare a cash flow statement, you need to have a general sense of the following daily operations:

- The amount of cash created or consumed by operations.
- The amount of cash invested in fixed assets.
- The amount of debt borrowed or repaid.

A cash flow statement requires information from your income statement. First, subtract all disbursements, such as operating expenses, labor costs, capital expenditure, and long-term debt (obligations that are not due for at least one year, e.g., bank debt or stockholder loans), from your beginning cash. Your cash receipts are obtained from daily operating activities, including all collections and interest earned from business accounts. The resulting figure is your net cash flow. If this number is positive, it indicates that the studio is self-sufficient in funding its cash flow needs. If this number is negative, it indicates that external funding may be needed to sustain the studio. The key indicator is the net increase/decrease in cash at the bottom of the statement, which represents the net result of operating activities. Without cash, a commercial recording studio will close.

Balance Sheet

The balance sheet is a financial picture of your studio at a particular date. It provides information on your studio by which you can measure change, primarily through your assets and liabilities. Figures used to compile the balance sheet are taken from previous balance sheets as well as current income statements.

Every company compiles a balance sheet at least once a year, often at the end of the calendar year covering January 1 to December 31. When constructing your balance sheet, include at the top of the page the legal name of the business, the type of statement, and the date.

Assets
The first section of your balance sheet should include your studio's assets. List anything of value that is owned or due to you. Assets are divided into two categories: current assets and fixed assets. These should be listed in descending order of liquidity.

Current assets include cash and other items that can be converted into cash within 12 months of the date of the balance sheet, such as:

- Money on hand, including petty cash.

- Demand deposits in the bank, such as checking accounts and regular savings accounts, plus temporary investments or marketable securities (stocks and bonds).

- Accounts receivable, or amounts due from customers in payment for services.

- Inventory and prepaid expenses, including office supplies and insurance protection.

- Long-term investments or assets, which are holdings you intend to keep for at least a year and yield interest or dividends. Examples are stocks, bonds, and savings accounts earmarked for special purposes.

Fixed assets are resources a business acquires for operations that are not intended for resale. Sometimes referred to as property, plant, and equipment, fixed assets include:

- Land (which on a balance sheet needs to show the original purchase price).

- Buildings and improvements.

- Equipment and furniture.

- Other tangible property used in running the studio.

Liabilities

In your balance sheet, liabilities are listed after assets. This is because they represent claims against the studio's assets. Liabilities may be current or long term and are listed in the order in which they will become due.

Like current assets, current liabilities consist of all debts, monetary obligations, and claims payable within 12 months. Typically they include the following:

- Accounts payable, or amounts owed to you for services purchased.

- Interest payable, which includes any fees due for use of both short- and long- term borrowed capital and credit extended to the business.

- Taxes payable, which includes amounts estimated by an accountant to have been incurred during the accounting period.

- Long-term liabilities are any payments, including mortgage payments, that are due 12 months after the date of the balance sheet.

Net Worth

Also called owner's equity, net worth is the claim of the owner(s) on the assets of the business. In a sole proprietorship, the owner's equity is under the owner's name. In a partnership, equity is each owner's original investment plus any earnings after withdrawals. For corporations, a net worth is given for the amount held by the shareholders.

On a balance sheet, total liabilities and net worth must always match.

Break-Even Analysis

The break-even analysis is a tool that indicates how much you have to sell to cover your costs with no profit and no loss. Once you pass this point your recording studio will create a profit. Since profit is dependent on sales volume, the price you set for your services, and the costs you incur in providing those services, your break-even analysis shows how these factors impact your profits. To estimate the break-even point you must separate fixed costs (such as rent and debt repayment) from variable costs (such as the cost of goods sold). Total variable costs are expressed as a percentage of sales.

The break-even formula (in sales dollars) looks like this:

$$\text{Break-even point} = \frac{\text{Total fixed costs}}{1 - \text{Total variable costs}}$$

For example, John opens his recording studio and estimates his total fixed expenses are about $10,000 for the first year. He estimates variable expenses of about $700 (expressed as a percentage, which in this example is 70 percent). So his break-even formula looks like this:

$$\text{Break-even point} = \frac{\$10,000}{1 - .7} = \frac{\$10,000}{.3} = \$33,000 \text{ approximately}$$

Therefore, John's recording studio must gross $33,000 to break even. This analysis provides John with a target amount he must generate to become self-supporting. Banks and lending agencies look carefully at break-even reports because they are concerned with the viability and capacity to service debt. Your job is to reduce this break-even amount and to show (if you prepare your break-even analysis on a monthly and yearly basis) that you can repay the loan during months in which the sales are greater than expenses.

Implementing Your Financial Plan

When you have accounted for all of the variables in your financial plan, it's time to put them into action. Often plans and reality clash, and what you expected to achieve and what you actually achieve are different. All your financial plans should have a completion date. This will ensure that you achieve your goals within a specific time frame. If you don't achieve your goals, you need to adjust your long-term plans.

In response to external or internal changes, you may need to make adjustments. You may be affected by changes in the marketplace, such as changes in customers' tastes, which you could not anticipate. You may be subject to technological or economic changes. As the manager of a recording studio you must react to these conditions. You should:

- Be alert to the changes in the recording industry, market, and customers.

- Check your financial plan periodically, determine what revisions are needed, and implement them.

Information that can help you act include business papers and trade magazines (see Resources), trade organizations, and general news items from newspapers, TV, or the Internet.

Writing a Business Plan

A business plan may be the most important document a recording studio owner puts together. A business plan serves as a blueprint for the operation, financing, and growth of your studio. Furthermore, a business plan is an essential communication tool that helps to convey your ideas to financiers, possible partners, and others involved with your studio. It is a living document that is used to gauge the success and progress of your business, and to determine if changes are required.

You need to write a business plan when:

- You are getting ready to start the business.

- You have defined the basic business concept.

- You have organized the service.

- You have chosen a location.

- You understand the financial position of the company.

Before you actually start writing your business plan, you should consider some of the important factors that affect your business. Many of these factors have been dealt with in your analysis of the general business environment. Your business plan should describe:

- The proposed product.

- The expected market.

- Strengths and weakness of the industry or environment.

- Financial aspects, including expected income and expenditures.

    Other important information you will need to collect:

- Résumés of founders and key management.

- Statistics related to sales and marketing.

- Potential customers and anticipated demand.

- Your direct competition.

- Financial information to support your studio.

- Newspaper articles about your business and industry.

- Regulations and laws that may affect your business.

Business plans need to be clear, logical, and systematic, and speak directly to your intended audience. Since this audience includes people who will sponsor your studio, you need to express your passion for your work, so that people will continue reading the document and investing in your ideas. Keep the document to approximately 20 pages, including a three- to five-page summary. Most business plans follow a set format:

- Cover page.

- Executive summary.
- Table of contents.
- Company description—mission statement.
- Industry/economic analysis, including growth rates.
- Market and competition.
- Strategies and goals.
- Products and services.
- Marketing and sales.
- Management and organization.
- Operations: officers and duties.
- Financial analyses, including a cash flow analysis, budget, net worth, fixed costs, flexible costs, and taxes.
- Summary.
- Appendix and supporting documents.

Cover Page
This identifying sheet contains your business name, address, and phone number; the principals (owners) of the business; and the date of publication. Since the cover page is the first thing someone will see, make sure you give it a professional look. If you have a studio logo, include it as a means of defining your company.

Executive Summary
The executive summary briefly describes (usually on one page) your company, its products and objectives, the environment in which it exists, and the studio's funding needs. Many investors will only read this section, so it is imperative that you capture their attention and explain your studio in this one page. The tone for the executive summary should be professional and businesslike, yet at the same time it should convey a sense of excitement.

There are many formats for an executive summary. One effective format is to present highlights of the business plan on a section-by-section basis. Many executive plans conclude on a personal note along the lines of, "The founders

Contents of an Executive Summary

1. Company name
2. Products
3. Market
4. Industrial trends
5. Projected market share
6. Management
7. Funding

of XYZ Studios are encouraged by the enthusiastic response from the market for our product." Another option is to include a personal assessment in a cover letter accompanying the business plan.

Although the executive summary appears first it should be written after the rest of the plan has been finalized. You should spend a good amount of time making this document as compelling as possible, since it may make the difference between someone funding your studio or not.

Table of Contents

A table of contents follows the executive summary. You should write this in outline form, with headings and subheadings. Include all page numbers in your contents, including those associated with the appendix.

Company Description/Mission Statement

A general description of your company should take no more than a few pages. Since other parts of the business plan present detailed information, this section addresses the company's objectives. For the purposes of funding, your projections should be succinct as well as specific, measurable, and achievable. Remember, this is an external document, not an internal management tool. Never make a projection that you know your company cannot deliver, because it will often be noticed right away by a professional reviewer of financial reports.

Your company description should include information on your company's history and founding and the products that it intends to sell or produce. All companies exist to accomplish some purpose, which should be expressed here in a measurable manner in a specific time frame. Highly abstract objectives are difficult for others to understand and won't attract funding. Keep in mind, too, that most investors want to know what they will obtain from their investment in a company.

A useful way to define the company's mission is to answer the following questions:

- What is our business?

- Who is the consumer?

- What is our value to the consumer?

- What will our business be?

- What should our business be?

Since companies and economies change, the mission statement of your studio should also change with the times.

Industry & Economic Analysis

An important step in writing the business plan is analyzing the industrial and economic conditions in which your studio exists. The aim is to produce a documented picture of the most significant environmental developments the company must consider. Changes in the external environment often require new company strategies.

An environmental analysis should answer two key questions: What are the major trends in the environment, and what are the implications of these trends for the company? These questions must be examined for each of the company's major environments, including:

- Public environment, including current trends and tastes in the music industry and how they affect your studio's short- and long-term viability.

- Larger or macro-environmental trends that may have an effect on the studio. These include economic, legal, and political environments that affect the operation of your studio.

Market & Competition Analysis

A market analysis explains who your customers are, why they need your product, and how your studio addresses these needs. Use your market segmentation (explained in the previous chapter) as proof of your research.

In this section you need to discuss your competition. You may want to explain your competitor's services, location, market share, price, and reputation. Discuss how your studio serves its market and how you have a competitive advantage over other studios.

Strategies & Goals

A strategic plan is for developing and maintaining a fit between your studio's goals and capabilities and its changing market opportunities. This section relies on your developing a clear mission and supporting goals. Establishing your strategies and goals will also help you research, analyze, and present your company to potential investors and partners and anyone who needs further information about your plans. Likewise, this section will help you select future markets, position your studio within these markets, and address competition.

Strategies are not simply bright ideas. A recording studio's strategy includes decisions about its current services and whether they need to be maintained, built upon, dropped, and/or re-created in the future. Strategies grow out of and are reflective of the environment in which you operate, the resources that you have or may be able to obtain, and the goals you set for yourself.

Each company has a set of potential goals from which to select. A recording studio might be interested in attracting better customers or increasing its market share, thereby increasing its profit margin. A studio cannot successfully pursue many goals simultaneously and should choose to emphasize certain ones. Your goals for the coming years should be stated in operational and measurable objectives. The general goal of "increased sales" should be expressed in a definable objective such as "increasing sales next year by 15 percent."

Products & Services

This section describes the recording studio's existing services and/or those that are planned. It is also a place for you to discuss any products in development or research plans, along with any relevant patents, copyright, and trademark issues. To support your case, include promotional materials such as catalogs, blueprints, and photographs.

Marketing & Sales

The marketing and sales section should cover the following areas:

- Target market. Identify the characteristics of this market and how you selected it through market segmentation. If possible, back up your discussion with examples from questionnaires, surveys, and research. If this is a new studio, state that you are making projections of market size. Most of this information will be gathered from the research described in chapter 2.

- Advertising. Show how your advertising will be tailored to your target market. Include rating sheets, promotional material, and timelines for your advertising campaign.

- Pricing. Pricing is a consequence of your market research and costing your product. Again, back up your information with materials from your research.

- Product. Explain what services your studio will provide.

Management & Organization

The company must have three elements to carry out its strategies: structure, people, and culture (mission). Your studio's organizational structure can be expressed as a management plan that identifies personnel in key positions. For all key managers you should include a current résumé. It may be to your advantage to explain what qualifies these people to run your studio, what their exact roles are, and how much time they will devote to the studio.

Summary

The summary of the business plan should consolidate your facts, reiterating the most important sections of the plan and expressing gratitude to the reader for taking the time to read the document.

Appendix & Supporting Documents

The appendix consists of records that back up the statements and decisions made in the business plan. The following items should be included:

- Personal résumés. Even if you are the sole operator of the studio you should include a résumé. Keep it to one page and include your working history, education, professional affiliations, and any special skills.

- Personal financial statement. If you are a new studio owner, include a statement of your assets and liabilities. This shows your current equity to possible investors.

- Credit reports. If you have established credit lines with wholesalers and suppliers, include them in your appendix. These reports act as a guarantee of your financial honesty. Also include reports from credit bureaus and banks.

- Legal documents. Include any papers relating to your legal structure, insurance, property, etc.

- Miscellaneous documents. Any other documents that are referred to but not included in the main body of your business plan.

Accountants, Lawyers & Insurance

Before we continue, we would like to emphasize the importance of retaining an accountant and a lawyer. Although this book is designed to make you a self-sufficient recording studio owner, these professionals will help you through the lifetime of your company.

A certified public accountant (CPA) keeps up with current changes in tax law and accounting processes, and helps you through tax time. Moreover an accountant can recommend the most appropriate accounting software for your company, advise you on investments, help you map out your personal and business financial future, and assist in obtaining loans.

Business lawyers are essential in operating a successful studio. They help you design contracts and offer legal protection of intellectual property (copyright, patents, and trademarks), bankruptcy, and other negotiable instruments (certificates of deposit, promissory notes, and commercial papers). The choice of a reputable lawyer begins with the legal society of your state, which can provide a list of lawyers in your area who would be suitable to your needs.

Chapter Summary

1. Recording studio owners need to understand the role of personal and business financial planning to operate a recording studio in the long term. This is achieved by using documents such as an income statement, cash flow statement, balance sheet, breakeven analysis, and business plan.

2. Budgets communicate planned income and assets for a specific period of time. Recording studio owners must control assets, expenses, and cash flow to meet current and future needs.

3. Liabilities are obligations created by borrowing or buying something on credit. Current liabilities most commonly associated with a new recording studio include accounts payable, notes payable, and accrued expenses. Owner's equity is what the owner possesses after liabilities are subtracted from assets.

4. A recording studio's profit (net income) is the amount after expenses are subtracted from revenues. Net income is represented in an income statement, which shows how the recording studio's cash was received and spent.

5. The balance sheet functions as a picture of a studio's financial position—its assets, liabilities, and owner's equity at a particular date.

6. The business plan describes the studio's mission, philosophy, and objectives and helps you put your plans into action and secure funding. Since this is an external document, the business plan should be written in a clear, interesting, and thorough manner. It should create an impression that the studio is a profitable and secure business run by responsible and talented people.

5. Financing Your Studio

After readying this chapter, you should be able to:
- Understand the various financial resources available to start a recording studio.
- Identify the four C's of credit.
- Explore alternative avenues of studio financing.

One of the major barriers for entry into the recording studio market is the lack of capital, or start-up money. If you do not have enough of your own money to start a business you may need to rely on some type of external funding.

In general there are two types of funding sources available for entrepreneurs: lending agencies and investors. Lending agencies include commercial banks, savings associations, and other financial institutions that engage in commercial lending. Investors, sometimes referred to as venture capitalists, are people or organizations looking for new businesses that have a potential of growth. Lenders are typically number driven in their analysis of a studio's potential. They focus on a recording studio's short-term potential, especially in loan repayment. Investors tend to look at the whole business and its long-term viability. It should be in your best interest to pitch your ideas in a different way to the two groups.

Commercial lenders also require from you a series of documents, including a well-written business plan (see the chapter on financial planning) with complete résumés of key employees. You also need to supply financial statements and proof of a legal business structure.

In lending money to potential recording studios, investors often look for a promise of a large rate of return. They are willing to accept more risk for the possibility of a big return. Lending agencies, on the other hand, tend to take a more cautious approach to lending money. They are looking for the ability of a recording studio to repay its debt, no matter how big the studio may be. When considering a loan request, lending agencies concentrate on four important characteristics, sometimes called the four C's of credit: character, cash flow, collateral, and contribution, or equity. (We will discuss each of these characteristics in detail below.)

Estimating your capital requirements is a two-step process. First, you need to calculate the amount needed to open your doors for business, commonly known as start-up costs. Start-up costs cover every item you must obtain, including equipment (such as computers and furniture), money for deposits, advertising, supplies, and inventory. Make a list of all the items needed, the date when they are needed, estimated total costs, and estimated up-front cash outlay. Try to minimize your actual cash outlay for start-up costs.

Once you've calculated the studio's start-up costs, you need to calculate the amount needed to cover operating expenses in excess of cash revenue up to your break-even point. This is known as your operating costs. Operating costs are the general expenses needed to run a recording studio. Examples include office salaries, rent, advertising, and utilities.

It is important that you do not underestimate the amount of money needed to start a studio. Let's consider some potential sources of funding.

Personal Savings

Personal savings are often the first source new recording studio owners use to finance their studio. Most investors will not risk their money if you do not put a certain amount of your own money into a project. Your savings may include checking accounts, savings accounts, stocks, and any liquid assets you can use to start a business.

If you own a home and have sufficient equity in the property, lenders are more willing to loan money. Compared to other types of loans, personal loans have the advantage of low interest rates over a longer period of time (10, 15, or 30 years). Another benefit is that interest up to $100,000 is an itemized deduction. If you place the proceeds in your studio, the loan is 100 percent deductible on your business schedule.

Many businesses funded by personal savings follow the strategy of bootstrapping. Simply put, bootstrapping means starting small and conservatively and controlling your expenses wisely. When the studio starts to turn a profit, you direct the profits back into the studio rather than into your own (or your partner's) pocket.

Banks & Financial Institutions

Banks are the next most likely source of capital. Commercial loans are heavily influenced by your ability to repay the loan as well as the personal impression you leave on the loan officer.

You should realize that most start-up companies do not secure loans from financial institutions. Banks make money on net interest income (the difference between what they borrow from depositors and the interest they receive) and therefore look for guaranteed investments. It is your job to prove to the banks that you can run a successful and profitable recording studio. Here is a list of criteria on which lenders typically base their decisions.

Character
The most subjective of the four C's of credit, character is based more on an individual rather than a business plan. A lender must have confidence in the individual running the

studio. Traits such as talent, honesty, experience, and reliability are pivotal in convincing a lending agency to part with their cash. To provide an objective view of a person's character, lenders use a credit history. Although the credit rating says little about a person's business savvy and planning, a good credit rating goes a long way toward convincing the lender that you can operate a business successfully and pay the monthly debt service.

Cash Flow

Banks need to be assured that the studio will have an adequate cash flow to pay its debt and operating obligations and still meet its other needs. Writing your first cash flow statement is a challenge, since projections are often less than perfect and lenders need to be assured that the margin of error has been considered and amply provided for. You should not only factor in interest and principal payment to the bank on a monthly basis, but you should be aware of industry trends and fluctuations.

Collateral

Lenders do not make their decisions solely on good collateral. However, they often try to obtain the best possible collateral on a loan, in most cases by securing liens or mortgages against tangible assets such as equipment or real estate. In many cases a lender requires a personal signature from the entrepreneur as additional security. This tactic compromises the principle of limited liability protection even if your business is a corporation.

Contribution

Before lending money to a business, lenders often require the entrepreneur to invest a significant amount of money to a project. This ensures that the entrepreneur is committed to the company's success and reduces the risk for a lender. This amount of equity required varies considerably depending on the industry. If the industry has a high success rate and the entrepreneur has good-quality collateral, the debt-to-equity ratio (also known as leverage) can be 3 to 1 or even 4 to 1. Due to all the variables involved in this decision, it is difficult to generalize on how much a business should contribute to a new studio venture. Some experts recommend a 2 to 1 ratio, which would mean that if you are seeking a $100,000 loan, you should have $50,000 of equity capital in the business.

Debt

Loans should be considered as debt. The length of time over which payments are due, or the term of debt, varies by lender. A lender can structure a loan so that the borrower has some latitude to amortize (pay off) the debt. Remember that the longer the loan term, the lower the monthly payment (principal and interest) will be. It is often a good idea to investigate if your lending agency will give you an initial moratorium on principal payments. This would allow you to build the studio before payments are due, especially when initial expenses are high. Moratoriums on principal payment usually last for no more than one year. If you fail to meet payments on the interest, this is considered to be a loan default, and you may be required to pay the principal on the outstanding amount immediately.

Loan Types, Rates & Rules

Loans are typically paid off in installments or balloon payments (a combination of installments with a final large payment). Loan offerings include:

- Revolving lines of credit. These are payable within a short period (for instance, one year) and are often for small amounts ($5,000–$50,000).

- Intermediate-term debt. Loans with terms of 60 months or less secured by collateral such as equipment.

- Term loans. These are used to acquire real estate and are typically amortized for up to 180 months. These can reach up to $100,000 for small businesses.

Regardless of how solid your recording studio is or how well it is performing, your rate of interest payment will fluctuate, because most business loans today are provided at a variable interest rate. This fluctuation is tied with the prime interest rate (the rate banks charge their "best" customers) on short-term loans. Also the rate is often associated with percentage points, which are a function of the risk level of the enterprise and other variables. Your interest rate may run anywhere from .5 percent to 2 percent, or as high as 3 percent or 4 percent, above the prime rate. This is why many financial institutions will not fund small loans. It is very difficult to get a commercial loan under $20,000, because the return on the investment is too low for the lending agency to gain a healthy return from the interest.

Lending institutions often have rules associated with lending that restrict an entrepreneur from making decisions without the lender's approval. It is a good idea to investigate the fine print dealing with these rules before making a decision to take a loan.

Finally, finance companies often loan money to projects that banks reject, but they charge higher interest rates and therefore should not be your first choice. As with banks, you should talk to several agencies to get the best rate.

Investors

The list of investors runs long in the business world, from your parents and friends to venture capitalists. Most investors in a new recording studio are found close to home, and they supplement the entrepreneur's own capital. The capital from these groups often comes from savings, marketable securities, and equity in homes via a second mortgage.

Friends and family are a good source if you are looking for small amounts of capital. Unlike financial institutions, they are more

Items to Include in a Loan Application

1. Cover letter
2. Cover page and table of contents
3. Loan amount and use
4. Description of your studio and its history
5. Your management team
6. Financial history of your recording studio
7. Financial projections
8. Your product
9. Personal financial statements
10. Any additional documentation (legal documents, product brochure, etc.)

likely to make a smaller, less risky investment. A drawback to using friends and family is that since they are not professional investors, they may not evaluate the potential of the studio, and your personal relationships could suffer if the studio fails. You should consider this possibility before pursuing such investments.

Professional venture capital fund managers tend to look for companies with high growth potential over the long term. They are interested in establishing limited partnerships whereby they supply the investment and remain as a silent partner. They look for high returns and investments that become liquid within relatively short periods. Venture capitalists also consider the character and experience of the entrepreneur and the management team, and seek out unique businesses that have an edge on the competition. They often associate themselves with companies that have patents, licenses, and trademarks. It is imperative that you present to potential venture capitalists a highly professional business plan.

Plastic Financing

If you cannot get a loan from a financial institution or find investors, you may need to rely on yourself to fund the recording studio. Many entrepreneurs turn to plastic financing as a means of starting a new business: They acquire several credit cards, then borrow to the card's limit to purchase goods or to obtain cash. This is certainly not a recommended method of obtaining capital, as most credit cards have rates of between 15 and 20 percent on unpaid balances. It can put you into debt very quickly and destroy your credit history as well as any chance of obtaining credit in the future. However, for those who require small amounts of money and have little or no assets, plastic financing is sometimes the only way.

Government Financing

There are numerous governmental sources of financing available to entrepreneurs. The best known is the Small Business Investment Corporation (SBIC), which not only supplies new companies with equity capital but extends unsecured loans to small businesses. The SBIC makes small investments in start-up companies through

Credit Laws

There are six important federal credit laws that you should be aware of:

1. Equal Credit Opportunity Act. This act prohibits discrimination in granting credit on the basis of race, age, sex, religion, marital status, or national origin.

2. Fair Credit Reporting Act. Requires credit bureau reports to contain accurate information and regulates access, review, and corrections.

3. Fair Credit Billing Act. Sets rules for credit card billing policies and administration.

4. Consumer Credit Protection Act. Requires disclosure of finance charges and annual percentage rates. This act also limits the liability of lost and stolen credit cards to $50 per card.

5. Fair Debt Collection Practices Act. Regulates and restricts the actions of debt-collecting agencies.

6. Fair Credit and Charge Card Disclosure Act. Requires information on fees, grace periods, and terms on credit and debit cards.

qualified Small Business Administration (SBA) loans. The Minority Enterprise Small Business Investment Corporation (MESBIC) invests in small businesses run by minorities. Both organizations have investment pools of private money that are leveraged with federal government funds via the SBA.

The SBA's primary purpose is to assist small businesses through financing at reasonable rates. An SBA loan is obtained through a regular bank loan, which is guaranteed up to 90 percent by the SBA if you default on the loan. The average SBA-backed loan is about $100,000, with an upper limit of $750,000, and has a maturity of up to nine years instead of the three to 30 years of a standard bank loan. Unfortunately, demand for SBA loans outstrips supply. Consequently, SBA loans are very difficult to obtain. It is a good idea to establish your studio and have some success before applying for an SBA loan.

Here are some of the loan programs offered by the SBA:

SBA 7(a) Loan Guarantee Program

This program provides loan guarantees up to $1 million or 75 percent of the loan amount. For loans less than $150,000, the SBA will guarantee up to 85 percent of the total loan. The SBA does this through various programs, including:

- LowDoc. The low documentation program is based on your credit history and your studio's cash flow. For loans of less than $50,000 you need only to file the appropriate SBA loan form. For loans up to $150,000, you must supply a copy of the completed application, along with tax returns for the previous three years.

- FA$TRAK. This program works for loans up to $250,000. The SBA guarantees 50 percent of the loan.

SBA Direct Loan Programs

- CAPLines. This program offers loans for capital projects on a short-term basis. There are several line-of-credit programs operating under the CAPLine heading. Each offers credit for labor, material, and capital costs.

- Microloan. The Microloan finances businesses through nonprofit intermediaries, and helps small businesses obtain loans ranging from $300 to $35,000. The program is ideal for companies that cannot obtain lines of credit.

- Certified Development Company (504 Loan). The 504 Loan program offers long-term loans for equipment and land and for interest on an interim loan. Terms are up to 20 years with low down payments.

- Small Business Investment Companies (SBICs) are companies licensed and regulated by the SBA that provide venture capital to start-up companies.

- One Stop Capital shops gather local, state, and federal agencies in one location to address the financial needs of small businesses.

Barter

Another way to help get a studio underway quickly and cost-effectively is through the long-standing tradition of barter: the exchange of goods and services with other companies and individuals. This is an open system that allows you to negotiate on any service. For example, one of your clients may be a certified public account who will trade recording time for accounting help. Recording studio owners often trade future studio time for goods and especially services. Many musicians and aspiring rock stars earn a living as carpenters, electricians, plumbers, or computer programmers.

Barter agreements can save you thousands of dollars and offer an initial influx of recording work that gives the studio some much needed early exposure. These sessions can also be useful for discovering and working out any kinks and determining a suitable workflow.

Chapter Summary

1. Capital is one of the greatest barriers for start-up recording studios. Your capital needs are based on two factors: start-up costs and operating costs.

2. Personal savings are often the first and easiest source of funding for a start-up studio. Home equity loans and bootstrapping are important for small businesses with limited funds.

3. Banks base their decision to lend money to an individual based on criteria including: your character, the collateral you supply, your studio's cash flow, and your contribution to a loan.

4. Venture capitalists only invest in businesses that offer a high return in a relatively short period of time.

5. Plastic financing (through credit cards) may seem a viable alternative to traditional financing, but the high interest rates charged by credit card companies place a heavy burden on personal finances.

6. Government agencies, such as the Small Business Administration, offer a range of grants for innovative small businesses and can help with other business needs.

6. Government Regulation

After reading this chapter, you should be able to:

- Understand the various federal, state, and local laws concerning recording studio operation.
- Obtain the correct licenses for your recording studio.
- Identify government programs that offer advice or financial assistance.

Often it seems that business and government are at odds with each other. But one of the government's objectives is to foster business prosperity on a national, state, and local level. Therefore, there are many governmental organizations that offer advice as well as financial support to recording studio owners.

Governments at all levels require companies to obtain various licenses and permits, and legislative bodies establish and administer specific laws about business practices. Some licenses and permits are expensive and take many weeks to obtain. For start-up recording studios, these requirements should be counted as start-up costs. Furthermore, it is crucial that you obtain these documents before spending time, effort, and money on your studio. If you later learn that your studio violates a specific code, you may incur heavy fines or have to close the business.

Federal Government

The federal government promotes competition through various federal agencies and legislation. The Sherman Antitrust Act and the Clayton Antitrust Act were designed to promote fair and equal trading and laid the groundwork for government intervention in business affairs. A consequence of these acts was the establishment of the Federal Trade Commission (FTC). The FTC acts as the government's watchdog group to monitor unfair business activities in the manufacturing, marketing, and sale of products. The FTC also regulates industry competition, especially the merger and acquisition of companies.

Other regulatory agencies created to protect consumers, employees, and shareholders from harmful actions of companies include:

- Equal Employment Opportunity Commission (EEOC), which regulates the hiring of staff and the workplace policies.

- Securities and Exchange Commission (SEC), which regulates stock exchanges.

- Occupational Safety and Health Administration (OSHA), which regulates workplace safety.

- Federal Communications Commission (FCC), which oversees radio and television broadcasts.

In addition, the federal government has passed other legislation affecting business activities:

- Americans with Disabilities Act (ADA), which requires employers to make accommodations for disabled employees.

- Fair Credit Reporting Act, which requires credit bureaus to report credit information in a fair and equal manner.

- Consolidated Omnibus Budget Reconciliation Act (COBRA), which requires employers to extend health insurance coverage.

- Fair Labor Standards Act (FLSA), which sets the minimum wage rate.

- Uniform Commercial Code (UCC), a legal guideline for business sales and contracts.

Finally, there are four federal government agencies that are important to recording studios:

- Internal Revenue Service (IRS), a division of the Department of the Treasury. The IRS controls revenue regulation and laws and is the federal government's collector of individual and corporate taxes. The primary tax issues that involve the IRS include: individual and corporate income taxes, excise tax (levied on businesses that have a national reach, such as air travel and telephone service), custom duties, tax credits, and deductions. The IRS is also a good source of information and documents dealing with taxation.

- Copyright Office. This federal agency ensures the protection of intellectual property.

- Patent and Trademark Office. This agency offers protection for inventions and brand makes.

- Small Business Administration (SBA). As noted earlier, the SBA helps small businesses gain funds via guaranteed loans.

State Government

State governments have also established legislation and created agencies to monitor businesses. Most of a state's revenue is derived from taxes levied on its citizens and businesses. These taxes include:

- Individual and corporate taxes. Apart from nine states, businesses must withhold this tax from employees' wages. Businesses are also required to pay state unemployment insurance and workers' compensation.

- Tax credits and deductions.

- Property taxes.

- Sales tax.

- Excise tax. These "sin taxes" are levied on gasoline, tobacco, and liquor and are often used to pay for public services such as road construction and education.

Most business-related licenses are issued via state government agencies. If your state assesses sales tax you need to obtain a resale permit. This will allow your recording studio to buy wholesale goods without paying tax, collect sales tax from customers, and submit the tax to the state agency on a regular basis.

Generally, the rules of establishing a business are controlled by each state. The process of business registration takes place through the secretary of state and in most cases requires the filing of appropriate documentation and payment of specific fees.

If you operate a vehicle as part of your business, you need to obtain a state vehicle registration and inspection sticker.

County & Local Government

Most cities and counties require businesses that operate within their jurisdiction to obtain a business license or certificate, whether your studio is full time or part time, is located at home or in a commercial zone, or has employees or not. When you have decided on your business structure you need to register an assumed or fictitious name with your local city or county clerk. A fictitious business name is any name that is different from the name of the individual, partnership, or corporation that owns the business. Each state has its own laws with regard to business names. Most require the owner to file within a period of time, usually around 30 days, of establishing the studio. This allows you to open bank accounts and also use the fictitious name for legal reasons. The paperwork is filed at the county clerk of the business's location. Name filings are often published in the local newspaper.

Local governments also regulate home occupancy. Generally, businesses cannot operate in residential zones. If you do plan to operate out of your home, check local laws to make sure your business qualifies. Restrictions are often based on the number of home businesses in a region, in order to control noise and traffic. It is a good idea to obtain a variance or condition-use permit. In certain areas these are not difficult to obtain as long as you can prove that your recording studio will not disrupt the character of the neighborhood. Other local ordinances include fire safety and building permits. Some cities have sign ordinances that restrict the size, location, and type of signage you can use.

Government Assistance

The federal government offers valuable information and assistance through the Department of Commerce. There are numerous offices within the department that can assist you with a wide range of services. Let's look at six agencies that may be of interest to a recording studio owner.

Bureau of Economic Analysis
This agency collects data on areas such as inflation, economic growth, regional development, and the world economy. This information is reported to the federal government and is available for businesses to use.

Census Bureau
Collected every ten years, the U.S. census offers a recording studio owner a wealth of important economic and social information. You can use census data on commerce, industry, and retail and wholesale operation to create marketing and business plans for your studio.

Minority Business Development Agency
The Minority Business Development Agency (MBDA) offers minority business owners an array of information and assistance in areas such as marketing, law, finance, and administration. This agency operates offices in major cities throughout the United States as well as smaller regional centers.

Office of Consumer Affairs
This advisor agency ensures that consumers' needs and interests are protected in the marketplace. OCA can also help businesses understand the needs of customers in their field. This agency works with federal, state, and local governments on improving their business markets.

Small Business Administration
As noted in the chapter on financing, the SBA offers information, advice, and loans to small business owners.

Service Corps of Retired Executives
SCORE is another valuable resource for your recording studio. Working and retired executive volunteers offer information on developing a business plan, securing financing, and managing business growth.

Chapter Summary

1. The federal government has created numerous agencies that regulate and monitor business activity in the U.S. Most agencies are designed to promote fair and equal trading within the U.S., as well as protect businesses and customers from unfair actions.

2. State governments collect taxes, issue licenses, and regulate business registration. County and local governments have jurisdiction over zoning laws and permits.

3. Federal government assistance is, for the most part, obtained from the Department of Commerce. The department has numerous agencies that help small businesses operate and grow in today's marketplace.

7. Studio Acoustics & Design

After reading this chapter, you should be able to:

- Understand the theoretical and practical elements underlying studio room acoustics.
- Outline studio needs regarding tracking and mixing spaces.
- Design and implement a studio with multiple rooms.
- Identify and troubleshoot acoustical problems.

When done properly, the acoustics of a studio can aid in capturing the tonal and spatial qualities that breathe life into a recording, and they allow the critical listening and evaluation necessary to craft a good final mix. When ignored or done improperly, the acoustics of a studio can downright sabotage attempts to capture good-sounding tracks and confuse the engineer by misrepresenting frequency balance and imaging. Poor acoustics make it extremely difficult to create a successful final product that will satisfy clients.

The purpose of this section is not to replace the input and skills of acousticians and/or contractors. It is to help studio owners and engineers understand acoustical concerns and get the most from their spaces.

More and more new studios are being started on very limited budgets, and while they may never have the acoustically inspiring spaces of some famous, high-end studios, they can also make great recordings with the proper approach and attention to utilizing their rooms. Before getting into the arrangement, treatment, and function of the various rooms in a recording studio, let's review some basic acoustic principles and phenomena. Following is a short list of terms and an outline of the major concepts. (See also chapter 2 for ideas on locations and electrical utilities.)

Basic Terms

Absorption: The reduction of sound energy in one medium, caused by either its transmission into another medium or conversion into another form of energy.

Acoustics: The behavior and/or perception of sound. The study of sound.

Decibels (dB): A logarithmic unit of measure for the level of sound or audio relative to a given reference. Decibels can be used to express levels of either acoustic or electric energy.

Diffraction: The bending or spreading out of sound waves around an object or through an opening. The lower the frequency of the sound, the greater this effect.

Diffusion: The scattering of sound reflections in many directions.

Frequency: The rate of cyclical vibration—in other words, how many times something vibrates through a repeating pattern in one second. The vibrating medium can be a great variety of things, including a guitar string, drum head, speaker, or air molecules. Frequency is expressed in hertz (Hz, cycles per second) and generally described as how high or low the sound is.

Frequency response: The relative sensitivity of an acoustic or electric system to sonic energy across a frequency range.

Sound pressure level (SPL): The measure of the acoustic force exerted upon a specific point. Inexpensive SPL meters are available through Radio Shack.

Wavelength: The distance between two corresponding points on successive cycles of a wave.

Reflections

Generally, when a sound wave comes in contact with a barrier or change in the medium of its transmission, some of its energy bounces back, some transitions into the new material, and some is lost (converted into another form). The sound that bounces back into the original medium is called a reflection. Since rooms often have hard boundaries (walls) that generally don't vibrate as easily as air, a lot of energy can be reflected. As sound waves continue to bounce around the room, they run into each other as well as the waves still emanating from the source. This interaction causes interference, both canceling and adding energy across the frequency spectrum in a pattern known as a comb filter. Because of this, reflections can cause drastic alterations to the frequency response of the room depending upon where the sound source and observer (listener) are within the space.

Because a reflection of a sound can reach a listener from a different angle than the sound coming directly from the original source, it can result in confusion as to the actual location of the source. Sound that emanates from the source and has not yet been reflected is called direct sound.

When a sonic wave front hits a dimensionally complex surface, it can scatter in multiple directions upon reflection. This effect is called diffusion. When sound has been scattered so much that its reflections appear random, coming from all directions, and too frequent to differentiate, it is said to have created a diffuse field.

Reverb

Reverb is the random series of reflections (diffuse field) of sound within an acoustic space. The time it takes reverb to lose 60 decibels of energy is called the reverb time (RT60). The actual length of this time (in seconds) is frequency-dependent and based on both the area and amount of sound absorption of the various materials in the room versus the total volume of the room itself. This is measured and/or calculated at specific frequencies.

Acoustic spaces have ranges of desirable and undesirable reverb times depending on their size and use. A lecture hall, for example, generally needs to have a much shorter reverb time (circa .4 to .9 seconds) than does a symphonic concert hall (up to 2.2 seconds). Larger lecture halls that were designed for maximum class enrollment are notorious for creating barely intelligible lectures. That is due to reverb times that are too long for speech. A chamber ensemble, on the other hand, might sound great in such a space.

Room Modes

Room modes (also called standing waves or resonant frequencies) are frequencies that are accentuated in some locations within a room but reduced in others. A modal frequency retraces the same path, in the same manner, as it bounces around a room because of the specific relationship between its wavelength and the distance it travels between reflective boundaries (usually walls). Strong modes are generally considered undesirable in studio situations, as they cause uneven frequency response either in the recording itself or in the perception of the mix in the control room.

Calculating some of the basic modes is rather simple. You can calculate the lowest frequency that will create a mode between two parallel walls by dividing the speed of sound (around 344 meters per second) by twice the distance between the walls.

The formula (where L = the distance between parallel walls, in meters), looks like this:

$$\frac{344}{2L}$$

Multiplying the result by 2, 3, 4, 5, 6, etc., generates the higher modes.

So, a room with parallel walls five meters apart will create the following five lowest modal frequencies (in hertz): 34.4, 68.8, 103.2, 137.6, and 172.

If an engineer were mixing in the middle of this example room, he may hear a great accentuation at 68.8Hz. In turn, he could decide to lower the level of the bass and/or kick drum. When played back later in another room, his mix may seem weak in the low end. Not cool.

So far, the modes discussed have occurred along only a single line (called axial modes). More complex modes can happen in a full two and three dimensions (called tangential and oblique modes, respectively). Since there are so many spatial possibilities, the various dimensions of the room frequently share modal frequencies. When this happens, the accentuation and cancellation of those frequencies can be further exaggerated.

Though the modes follow a linear progression in ascending order from low to high, the ratios between successive modes gets smaller, as does our perception of the distance between them. Ultimately, modal behavior at the higher frequencies becomes compacted, with very small areas of constructive and destructive interference that start to average out. This means that the most problematic modal frequencies are generally the lower ones.

General Considerations

Before considering the acoustics of the rooms within a recording studio, ask yourself these questions:

- What sort of work will be the specialty? (Bands, voice-overs, artist demos, pianists, mastering, post-production…)

- What styles of music will be most prevalent? (Klezmer, hip-hop, rock, classical…)

- How large will the ensembles be? (Solo artists, four-piece rock combos, jazz septets, studio orchestra…)

- What sort of spatial or financial limitations are there?

- Is the studio a converted garage or an industrial space?

- How should the floor plan and utilities be configured?

While it's great for a studio to specialize in a particular kind of recording, you don't want to have too small a market. The physical layout and acoustics of a studio should allow for various applications and diverse clientele. One client may only need MIDI production and a single-microphone vocal track, while another has a five-piece combo plus a horn section, requiring many rooms and two dozen microphones. Still others may not require any mics at all, just line inputs or a high-quality set of computer software plug-ins for mastering.

Each room in a studio has a particular function and should have different acoustic properties. Considerations of reverb time, first-order reflections, modes, and sonic isolation are dependent on function. Following is an outline of the studio rooms, their sonic goals, and some suggestions for achieving those goals through design and acoustic treatments.

The Control Room

The control room is where all critical listening and mixing occurs. Many important recording decisions are made here, based upon what the engineer hears. Whenever possible, the control room should have easy and fast access to all tracking rooms.

Acoustically, the control room should be clear and flat in its frequency response. More than any other space in the studio, sonic accuracy must be the goal. A sound's perceived location in space (imaging) should be easily perceived. Generally, the reverb time should be from .3 to .45 seconds, close to that of a typical home living room.

The primary obstacle to a flatter frequency response in the control room is room modes. To combat these, many different techniques are employed.

Figure 7.1: Small control room. Courtesy of Digidesign, a division of Avid Technology, Inc.

Figure 7.2: Large control room. "Squid Hell" courtesy of Alactronics.

Avoid the Parallel

First, avoid axial modes (usually the strongest) by eliminating major parallel surfaces. If possible, opposite walls should angle in opposite directions by a total of five degrees or more. Typical 90-degree angles and parallel walls are a big no-no.

Angling the front wall, so that it is not parallel with the back, has two main positive results. It avoids the axial modes that would be created and also reflects the sound coming from the speakers away from the listener, which helps to clear up the interference and temporal issues. Frequency response, clarity, and imaging may all be enhanced by angling the front wall. This is usually accomplished by dividing the wall into sections, angled left and right, and/or by sloping it toward the floor or ceiling.

Angled Panels & Diffusers

A similar, yet less drastic way to stop modes from forming is by using angled paneling or simple diffusers to scatter reflections. When placed along the center of walls, angled panels can thwart some resonances. This method is not as effective as angling the walls themselves, and the diffusers may exacerbate other problems depending on where they are placed.

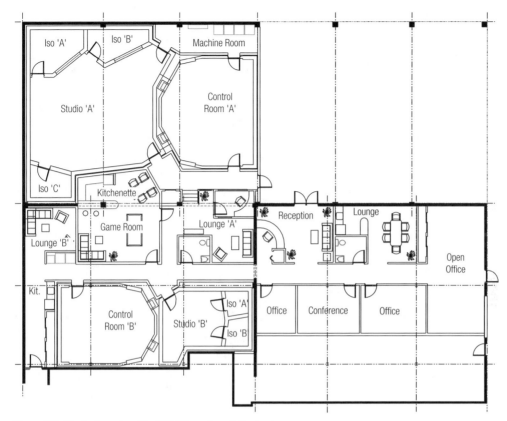

Figure 7.3: Studio floor plan. "Squid Hell" courtesy of Alactronics.

Figure 7.4: ArtDiffusor Model C. Courtesy of Acoustics First.

Room Ratios

X	Y	Z
1	1.14	1.39
1	1.17	1.47
1	1.26	1.41
1	1.26	1.59
1	1.28	1.54
1	1.45	2.10
1	1.47	1.70
1	1.60	2.33
1	1.62	2.62

Room Dimensions

Relative room dimensions also play a major role in the formation of tangential and oblique modes, as well as determining which of the many modes created will overlap in frequency. One way to avoid exacerbating these problems is by making the ratios between the dimensions mathematically more complicated. If they are related by simple integer ratios, then they will share modes. The room's length, width, and height should definitely not be the same or multiples of each other, or even share a simple common denominator!

Some recommended and popular ratios are given in the chart. Though most often x, y, z here are used as height, width, and length, the room dimensions do not need to follow that ordering. There are great-sounding studio control rooms that are wider than they are deep.

Absorption

A final popular method for stopping unwanted modes from forming is by removing the particular areas of reflection for offending frequencies. There are several ways to do this. Materials that absorb the specific modal frequencies can be added to the surfaces they must bounce off of to be created. Many companies make different types of foam, fabric, fiberglass, vinyl, and rubber absorbers for these purposes. Some even custom-manufacture requested shapes and sizes to accommodate users' styles and colors, as well as frequency needs.

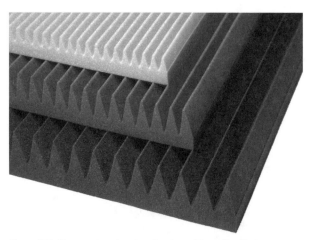

Figure 7.5: Foam wedge absorber. Courtesy of Acoustics First.

When looking to purchase and implement such acoustic treatments, you should know exactly which frequencies need to be removed, to what degree, and at what locations. Each type of absorber has a specific frequency response, published by the manufacturer. The amount of absorption, expressed as a coefficient, is plotted across numerous frequencies. This absorption coefficient can be seen as the percentage of sound energy (at a specific frequency) that will be removed from the room when it hits the absorber. For example, an absorber with a .23 coefficient at 500 Hz will remove 23 percent of the energy at 500Hz from any sound hitting it; 77 percent of the energy is reflected back into the room. If an axial room mode at around 500Hz is relying on this surface to keep reflecting back and forth, it will lose 23 percent of its energy each time it hits. For a room that's 5.5 meters wide, the room mode would reduce by 23 percent around 31 times. That would remove all but 1 percent of the energy in about half a second.

When reading absorption coefficients, you should keep in mind that they are published by the people trying to sell you the products. There are many ways to measure or calculate these numbers, which can vary the results quite a bit, and manufacturers are free to use whichever methods they want. There are no enforced standards for these tests. Many products advertise coefficients of greater than 1, which looks great but is a particularly confusing claim. It can be seen to imply that the amount absorbed is greater than the amount that goes in! Generally, these kinds of numbers are based on including the energy loss from the sides of the absorber, or by hanging it freely in space (where all angles can absorb). When taking measurements, other companies mount absorbers in a fashion more closely simulating how the materials will actually be used. Due to these discrepancies, when fitting a product to your individual needs, the relative frequency contour of absorption is often more useful than the actual claimed coefficients.

Trapping

When dealing with the low end of the frequency spectrum, it is sometimes more effective to use resonating traps than traditional absorbers. Traps are enclosed spaces that are designed to set up strong modal resonances at specific frequencies. When traps are placed in areas where room modes are strong, a lot of their energy enters the trap space. The energy that resonates within the trap tends to bounce around inside and weaken. A number of acoustics companies make movable traps that can be placed around the room where needed.

Low-Frequency Interference

The reflection of low frequencies from the near-field monitors off of the front wall can cause interference problems just as severe as those caused by room modes. In fact, these reflections are often more frequency specific and obvious due to their simplicity. The problem is that lower frequencies have such long wavelengths (slow cycle times) that when the sound travels from a speaker to the front wall, and then back again to pass the speaker and head for the listener, a whole cycle may not yet be completed. Just as with modes, accentuation of some frequencies occurs while others are cancelled. To keep this from happening, many studios make the front wall very absorptive and employ bass trapping.

Figure 7.6: Tube Traps bass absorbers. Courtesy of Acoustic Sciences Corporation.

Imaging

As mentioned above, being able to accurately hear where sounds are placed in the stereo or surround fields is extremely important when crafting a final mix. The primary obstacles to accurate imaging are, once again, first-order reflections. The mix engineer needs to hear direct sounds from the speakers as the strongest, without competition from reflections off the side walls in particular. Generally, studios use either foam absorbers to soak up some of this sound or angled panels to redirect it.

Both panels and absorbers can be installed easily by two people with the help of a simple hand mirror. One person sits at the primary listening/mixing position while the other stands at the wall with the mirror. The second person holds the mirror flat against the wall, with the glass facing out, and moves it around until the person at the mix position sees the speakers in the mirror. That is where the absorbers should go. If panels are being used, you can again use a mirror to determine where the sound reflections are being sent. Before doing either of these things, you must be certain the monitor speakers are in their best and final positions. Changing speaker or listener positions will change where the absorbers or panels should go.

Both wall-mounted and near-field monitoring are discussed in chapter 8, so I will simply make some notes on positioning here. What many people don't realize when placing speakers, especially near-fields, is just how prevalent first-order reflections can be. Besides wall, ceiling, and floor reflections, sound from the speakers can bounce off of objects such as mixing boards, furniture, computer monitors, and even tape machines. Each of these can cause interference issues, complicate imaging, and reduce sonic clarity. Reducing the intrusiveness of these objects and modifying angles can help reduce these problems. The mirror comes in handy here as well.

Symmetry

In a control room, it is a good idea to have each side of the room be as close to a mirror image of the other as possible. The speakers and mixing equipment should be centered between the side walls. The monitor speakers should be facing the engineer so that the speaker cones, ribbons, and horns are facing him/her directly. When the aspects of the room, speakers, and the listening position are not symmetrical, they can throw off not only the imaging but the perception of balance and frequency response. Critical and precise mixing in such an environment can be very difficult.

Mechanical Vibrations

An often overlooked aspect of studio design is the reduction of miscellaneous mechanical vibrations. In all studio rooms the walls, lighting, furniture, and equipment must be securely fastened and sturdy enough not to vibrate. It can be disconcerting and distracting when furniture or lighting fixtures buzz or rattle in the control room. In the tracking rooms, such as the live room or booth, these extraneous sounds can sometimes make getting a good take nearly impossible. Try to minimize these vibrations beforehand, listening carefully for them under various conditions and SPLs, and deal with them as soon as they come to your attention.

Reverb Time

As mentioned at the beginning of this section, controls rooms are typically best with a reverb time from .3 to .45 seconds. For small rooms, it may not be easy to achieve times that long! If absorption is used to minimize reflections, improve bass response, stop the more problematic modes, and improve imaging, then the decay of energy in the room will be much quicker. In smaller control rooms, especially those under 6,000 cubic feet, it is especially important not to overabsorb. Use the alternative means mentioned above to combat these acoustical issues.

Another way to increase the perceived reverb time is to place diffusers along the back wall. They help reduce modes without absorption and also lend a sense of space. Larger spaces tend to be more diffuse, so we relate these two factors in our perception.

Figure 7.7: ArtDiffusor Model E. Courtesy of Acoustics First.

You can measure reverb time using inexpensive acoustics software (such as the ETF 5 or AudioTester), handheld measurement tools, or good 24-bit recording equipment and software. On your DAW or multitrack, begin by placing a loud ½-second burst of white or pink noise on one track at one second into the session. Set up a microphone in the listening position and prepare to record it to another track, but don't bus it to the speakers until the recording is completed and *record-enable* is turned off (otherwise it could feed back in a serious way). Calibrate your monitoring and the mic/preamp so that the white noise provides a very loud sound (at or above 100dB SPL…*ouch*) in the room without overloading any part of the system. *Before you start, be certain your speakers can handle this!* The levels on the digital record track should be set to read a steady –5dB. Record the burst and a few seconds after. In the software, use the zoom function to see the amplitude of the waveform. When it gets down to where the waveform peaks are at –65, determine the session time. Subtract 1.5 seconds, and you have the reverb time.

If the reverb time of the control room is too long, absorptive and trapping techniques can be used to bring it down. Start by placing only the absorption that needs to be there for the other studio purposes previously mentioned. Adding a rug or two can also really help bring the reverb time down.

Measuring Frequency Response

The inexpensive software solutions and handheld acoustics devices mentioned above can also be used to determine the frequency response of the room/monitor combination. Of course, the do-it-yourself approach can also work here. If your software DAW has an automatable oscillator using a control graph on one channel, automate a very slow sweep from 20Hz to 20kHz. If it does not have such a function, create 3-second sine tone bursts at frequencies starting at 20 Hz and continuing in steps of 10 percent increase in frequency until you reach 20kHz. This will be around 100 steps and five minutes in length, but pretty darn accurate. Calibrate the outputs so that the SPL of the 500Hz sine tone in the room is around 90dB at the mix position. As in the reverb example, set up a microphone with a good, strong recording level (around −16dB this time), but don't bus it to the outputs yet. Record the sweep through the mic (you will probably want to leave the room for this one). When done, zoom in and measure the amplitude (in dB) at the middle of each recorded step. Accurate LED-style level meters, with added .5dB-stepped (or less) numerical displays, will also help tremendously. Plot the findings on a graph or write out the series. This is the unweighted frequency response of the room, equipment, and speaker combination.

EQ

After all acoustic considerations and treatments have been exhausted, many studios carefully add EQ between the mixer's monitor outputs and the amp/monitor speakers. Fine EQ adjustments are added in exact opposite relation to the final frequency response measurements. All adjustments, however, should also be considered in relation to perception as well as careful listening to various published audio CDs you are very familiar with. Special care should be taken with frequencies below 80Hz, especially if there is no subwoofer in the system. Cranking 30Hz in the EQ to compensate for speakers that were not meant to go much lower than 65Hz is not a good idea. You can damage your new speakers, reduce their useful life span, and reduce their fidelity. This EQ is used primarily to offset the room, not the speakers. It's also important to note here that the sound is being specifically crafted for the mixer's position (the sweet spot), and it may or may not be clear or flat in another position.

Other Construction Concerns

Double Walls

To help keep the sound from leaking between rooms, most studios employ a double wall construction. Simply put, there are two walls separating all the rooms. From the control room there is an interior wall, several inches of space, and then another outer wall (the interior wall for the live room or booth). This spacing is to keep sound from translating into mechanical vibrations through the wall and then becoming sound again on the other side. With two walls the sound must become acoustic, mechanical, acoustic, mechanical, and then acoustic to get through; energy is lost in each transition, lowering the amount that makes it all the way through. Insulation can be placed loosely between the walls to absorb even more sound. Rubber or vinyl barriers can also be strung in between. All spaces between the floor and the bottom of the wall must be caulked so that sound cannot pass under the walls. Often, two or three layers of thick drywall are hung on the interior of each room. Additionally, care must be taken so that the sound cannot travel easily between rooms through the ceiling or the floor itself. Support beams should not go through both rooms but across each room individually. All air spaces in the ceiling should be well insulated. Plumbing and ductwork should not move directly from one room to the next (more on this later).

Floating Floors

To keep sound from moving mechanically through the floor structure, studios with a few dollars often *float* one or more of their floors. This is done by separating the room's floor from the subfloor by way of thick neoprene (rubber) feet or slabs. Neoprene does not transmit vibrational energy well, so little can move between floors through mechanical vibrations. To maximize this vibrational decoupling, the entire room is often built and floated so that it does not connect to the outer, larger room or structure in any direct way. Sometimes, large springs are also used to float spaces.

Windows

To help the engineer keep track of what's happening with players, mics, and equipment, and to aid in communication with and between the players, everyone should be able to see each other during the session. This means there should be a window between the booth and live room as well as between the control room and those rooms. Studios often have one large window looking out to both areas from the control room. In smaller studios, if there can only be one window, then it should go between the booth and live room. The players must see each other!

So, along with double wall construction and the idea of decoupling comes double-paned (or sometimes quadruple-paned) windows. One side should be made from ⅝-inch plate glass and the other from ¾-inch glass to discourage similar types of resonances. If you're on a budget or constructionally challenged, you can purchase high-quality fixed-pane windows from a home improvement store. One windowpane (or two, if you're using double-paned, prefabricated windows) is placed in each wall. The sills do not touch but are joined by a neoprene gasket around the entire interior area. Each pane is, in turn, floated from the sills by thick neoprene stripping. Everything must be well caulked to ensure an airtight seal. This decouples the windows and panes from each other and makes the entire window structure airtight. Just like the walls of the control room, the windows should be angled at five or six degrees total to avoid modal resonances between glass panes.

Sound Locks

To go along with the double walls and double windows, double doors (called a sound lock) are necessary as well. These are extra heavy and hung to latch firmly, with gaskets all the way around to seal everything well. With a flashlight and all lights off, you should see no light through the sides, top, or bottom of a closed door.

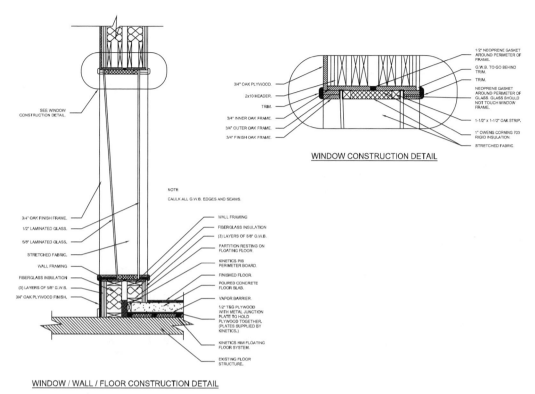

WINDOW CONSTRUCTION DETAIL

WINDOW / WALL / FLOOR CONSTRUCTION DETAIL

Figure 7.8: Window/wall/floor construction methods. Courtesy of Alactronics.

Ventilation

After acoustic treatments, double walls/windows/doors, and entire floating rooms, there can still be tremendous sound leakage from the ventilation. So why not just remove it? Because you just built airtight rooms in which to place crazy, flailing drummers for hours on end. People just might pass out from the lack of oxygen (or the smell).

Minimizing ventilation noise, however, is an expensive and space-consuming endeavor. The best air conditioners for studio purposes are fairly large, industrial, external units, specially designed to be quiet. They should not touch the exterior walls of the building directly. Ductwork should be extra large, changing dimensions often and with all seams assembled smooth (so they don't create whistling noises). The ducts should also incorporate a few larger chambers (of various sizes) lined with sound absorptive materials. Inlet and outlet(s) should not be directly opposite each other. The changing dimensions and volume keep modes from building up in the ducts, while the chambers help trap and absorb the noise that does occur.

Electrical Issues

Chapter 2 outlined some of the primary considerations for electrical utility and basic wiring. Let's reiterate some key points and add a few new ones.

Studio wiring should be 12-gauge Romex connected to 20-amp breakers. All audio devices should be on a separate breaker from lighting, fans, or any other nonaudio electrical items. In addition, they should be on opposite sides (legs) of the breaker panel. Audio circuits should also come at the top of the breaker, where the service line first enters. The ground for all audio circuits should go directly to earth, not the pipes or any unknown ground. A metal post can be sunk outside for this purpose. Use a licensed electrician.

No fluorescent bulbs or dimmers of any kind should be used in the studio. Both can cause hum in the audio signal.

The power for all equipment should be conditioned (maybe even regulated) and connected to a central UPS (uninterruptible power supply). Everything should be surge and spike protected with a warning if there are any grounding problems. Voltage and amp metering is also useful—and the lights look cool in the control room.

Audio Wiring

Audio cabling must be run from room to room, with connection panels on each end. This makes hooking everything up for tracking much more convenient. Generally, studios run PVC piping through the walls and run the multicable snakes through that. The PVC should be stuffed with insulation in a number of places along its path, so the rooms remain sonically isolated from each other.

Audio wiring should be kept far away from lighting and light switches, as well as power outlets and power lines in the walls. In addition, power cables should never be coiled or run parallel to audio. If audio and power cables must cross, they should do so at a 90-degree angle so as to minimize exposure. For more on cabling and connections, see chapter 8.

Isolation Booths

An isolation booth is a smaller space that is designed to offer the most isolation from outside noise and other instruments playing. It is generally the quietest of all studio rooms, with the least reverb or reflections. This space should definitely be acoustically treated so as to have no obvious modal resonances. You can either construct an iso booth from scratch, buy one prefabricated, or modify an existing space. This last option is generally the cheapest, but least effective.

When constructing a booth, employ the techniques discussed above for double walls, window, ceiling, and floating floor. Treating the ventilation is especially important here as are placement of electrical outlets and lighting issues.

Fortunately, many prefabricated booths come with doors, windows, sonic isolation, and ventilation issues already addressed. Many are modular and come in pieces designed for easy assembly, relatively speaking. Using one of these, and placing it within the larger live room, may be more expensive than building a booth (if you do the work yourself). They do save lots of time and aggravation, however, in addition to being quite effective.

When on a shoestring budget, you can modify a closet or small pre-existing room to act as a booth. Generally, isolation will not be great…but claustrophobia may be. Another drawback to these spaces is the lack of visual cues, as they often don't include a window.

Figure 7.9: Isolation booth. Courtesy of the University of Massachusetts Lowell.

To make the frequency response of booths more even (without a lot of modes or reflections) they are often treated with a lot of absorptive materials. Some people who prefer a little more spatial context in the recording treat only one of each opposing wall with absorbers. If you use this approach, you must take special care not to create too much comb filtering. The exact placement of performer and microphone becomes more critical (see chapter 14 for more on this).

Amp Closets

In order to maximize the number of isolated spaces available in a studio (and allow for the ridiculously loud levels some guitarists use to get the tone they like) many studio engineers like to place the amplifiers in broom closets, close the door, and record them in there. Because of this practice, more and more studios either wire closets with microphone connections and instrument tie lines, or build dedicated mini isolation booths. These *amp closets*, as they have come to be called, can be placed almost anywhere and don't have to be much larger than the amps themselves. To be most effective, however, they should include a fair amount of absorption or other protection from the effects of first-order reflections. In addition, since they are housing amplifiers generating high SPLs, they should be well isolated, either by physical space (for example, if the studio is on the second floor and the amps are in the basement) or by acoustic treatments. This small investment in space and equipment can be a very useful addition to any studio. Prefabricated units are also available.

Note that because of their limited size, amp closets are really designed for close-miking techniques. Acoustically, they have higher modes and critical frequencies, and very short reverb times.

Live Rooms

The largest of all tracking rooms, the live room is a space where multiple performers can fit at one time and the acoustics have the feel of a small concert hall. The reverb time of a live room is greater than the others, in the range of .65 to 1.4 seconds. If possible, this reverb level should be accomplished with minimal modal resonances but not much in the way of absorption (unless the room is *huge*). Materials used on the surfaces should be mostly reflective. Complexity of room geometry and reflective surfaces often works well. Throw rugs and blankets should be available to control reflections and modify the reverb time as needed. In addition, you can modify the acoustics of the space with movable partitions (called gobos) designed to either absorb or redirect sound by reflection (more on their use in chapter 14).

Figure 7.10: Tracking (or live) room. Courtesy of the University of Massachusetts Lowell.

Building a Gobo

Gobos can be ordered, but are relatively simple and inexpensive to build. The ones outlined below are light and very easy to store and offer great absorption. With a quick trip to local hardware and fabric stores you can purchase the necessary items to build these very useful studio tools. The following items are needed.

- Tools: hammer, work gloves, staple gun, box cutter razor blade, electric drill with screw bit, electric table or miter saw, pencil, and tape measure.

- From hardware store: construction-grade two-by-fours; unfaced R19, 16-inch center insulation (flame retardant); three-inch drywall or wood screws; and staples for staple gun. (Note: Rockwool with plastic sheathing, from US Gypsum, or rigid fiberglass panels, such as Owens Corning 703, can be substituted for the unfaced R19 insulation. Both are less likely to shed fibers into the air or onto the skin. Both, however, are also more expensive.)

- From fabric store: industrial burlap (usually sold in yards) in your color of choice.

Before you begin shopping, draw out the height, width, and number of gobos needed for your particular studio needs and working methods. If unsure, a good start might be to create four small ones for guitar amps (36 inches high by 32 inches wide) and two large for drums and vocals (72 inches high by 48 inches wide). The materials will only cost around $175 total depending on the color of the burlap. (For some reason color can increase the price up to $2 per yard.) You can always build more at another time; just make sure you have enough space to store them when they're not in use.

You are basically building a small, movable, self-standing wall with a 16-inch center. When planning or measuring before you build, make sure the width is a multiple of 16 inches just like a normal studded house wall. This allows the proper fitting of the insulation.

As an example, when building a small gobo with the dimensions listed above, you would need 190 inches of construction-grade two-by-fours. This allows for 32-inch top and bottom boards (horizontal width), three 36-inch-long boards for the vertical supports, and two nine-inch boards for feet. Here are the basic steps.

Build the frame as you would a wall, and screw all the two-by-fours together using two three-inch drywall screws per spot (use the following diagrams as guides).

Wearing work gloves so as not to get itchy, measure and cut the open-faced insulation to 36-inch lengths with the razor. (Cut the insulation on top of a two-by-four to avoid dulling your blade.)

Lay the pieces of insulation between the vertical boards and staple them in place with the staple gun. If the staples are not completely flush, use a hammer to drive them in the rest of the way.

For the feet, cut two nine-inch lengths of two-by-four and attach them with drywall screws to the bottom board at a 90-degree angle. They should be a few inches in, at the outsides of the 32-inch bottom frame board.

Once framing and insulation are completed, wrap the gobo with the industrial burlap, pulling tightly and stapling to the frame. Again, if the staples are not flush, use a hammer to drive them in the rest of the way. Make sure the insulation is completely covered by the burlap.

These homemade gobos work well and look great. To allow greater flexibility in use, you can add pressed board to cover one side (under burlap). This creates one side with absorption and one with reflective capability.

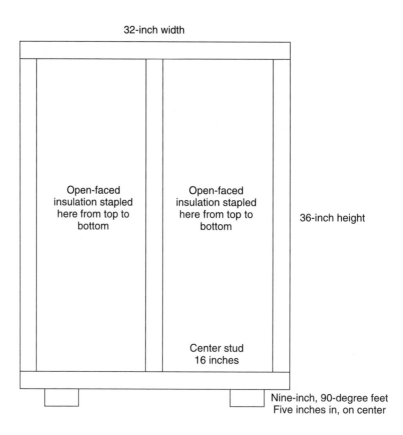

Figure 7.11: Gobo frame front view

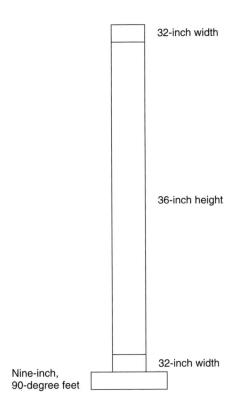

32-inch width

36-inch height

32-inch width

Nine-inch,
90-degree feet

Figure 7.12: Gobo frame side view

Chapter Summary

1. Long before you order any equipment, you must secure a suitable studio location. This location must pass all noise and utility criteria described in chapter 2.

2. A floor plan outlining all rooms, their intended purpose, acoustical considerations, and approaches to acoustical treatments is paramount and should be made early.

3. Properly designed and implemented acoustics are essential in the making of great recordings. To design your studio space and address problems, you need to understand room modes, reverb times, reflections, sonic interference, and isolation techniques.

4. Initial consideration should be given to the avoidance of room resonances. Avoid parallel surfaces and use proper room dimensions, along with traps, diffusers, angled panels, and absorbers, to remove these sonically destructive phenomena.

5. The various rooms within the recording studios serve widely different functions and, therefore, have distinct acoustical concerns and personalities. All of them are ideally mode-free, but each has drastically different requirements for reverb time and reflections.

6. Moveable acoustic treatments such as blankets, pillows, throw rugs, and gobos are essential in even the best spaces.

8. Equipment & Supplies

After reading this chapter you should be able to:
- Understand the theoretical and practical elements of recording equipment.
- Outline complex audio and synchronization signal flow.
- Design and implement a complete professional recording system.
- Troubleshoot problems with equipment integration.

The current state of recording technology is both exciting and confusing. While the advances of the newer equipment offer greater power and versatility in working methods, for any one studio task there may be anywhere from ten to thousands of choices of manufacturers and models of gear. Not only is it difficult to choose among all these options, but determining how best to integrate all the necessary pieces can become quite a puzzle.

On the other hand, as the technology has become more sophisticated, it has also become less expensive. These days, professional-level recording studios can be started with as little as $25,000 in audio equipment.

The following sections discuss both the theory and function of the various pieces of gear necessary for multitrack recording, and provide guidelines for outfitting a professional studio. Specific device choices are a matter of personal preference and working style, and so are left up to you. Keep in mind while reading that the quality of the final product depends on a combination of equipment, how it's integrated, and (most important) the expertise and creativity with which it is used. In the end, the technology is just a tool. You control it—don't let it control you. Your gear should be quick, relatively simple, and easy for *you* to work with.

Recording Platforms

There are two main types of recording technology in use today, analog and digital. While there are still proponents of analog recording, digital has become much more cost effective as well as more flexible and powerful. Since the final delivery format of most recordings is also digital (usually CD, SACD, DVD, or MP3), digital technology is where most new studios should concentrate their resources.

Digital audio recording platforms also come in two main varieties, tape and hard disk. Several very good tape-based MDMs (modular digital multitracks) are still on the market today, but hard-disk systems are cheaper, have more features, higher track counts, and are more easily expandable. In addition, there are more DAWs (digital audio workstations) on the market and fewer tape-based platforms with every passing day.

DAWs are either stand-alone units or based around a computer. The latter variety requires a separate computer to act as a host to the DAW's particular hardware/software combination. This setup allows you to upgrade and configure your system in countless, open-ended ways. In addition, these DAWs offer a familiar interface and expanded functionality, allowing users to print, burn CDs, surf the net, e-mail, update databases, keep client records, edit video and pictures, or handle any other general computer-aided task.

The greatest drawback to the computer-based DAW is compatibility. Since there are so many variations in the configuration of system hardware and software, conflicts and incompatibilities are common. A few helpful audio manufacturers test their products with most popular computers, operating systems, and storage technologies and publish their findings on the Web. Even so, there is always a lag time between the release of a new platform or technology and thorough testing, which makes it hard for manufacturers to keep up. With the infinite combinations possible it is also difficult to guarantee that a particular one will work properly. Additionally, computer DAWs are susceptible to viruses, especially PCs. Virus protection software is a must and should be updated consistently.

Stand-alone DAWs, on the other hand, are comparatively fixed in design and architecture. While this does limit their functionality and upgradability, they do what they are designed to do both consistently and well.

Audio Interfaces

An audio interface is a hardware device that is added to a computer to expand (and/or upgrade) its audio input and output capabilities (I/O). While many computer models boast built-in, high-fidelity audio functionality, the sound inputs and analog-to-digital (A/D) converters on computers or consumer sound cards are not of high enough quality to make professional recordings, nor can they appropriately interact with professional balanced microphones. Sound output by these means is also not of high enough quality for accurate monitoring or duplication. An external interface must, therefore, be added. This interface can connect to a laptop using the USB or Firewire (IEEE-1394) ports on most new computer platforms, or by means of proprietary connections to PCI or PCMCIA (CardBus) cards added to the computer. There are many types and configurations on the market today.

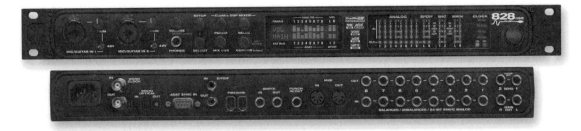

Figure 8.1: Mark of the Unicorn 828mkii audio interface.

Figure 8.2: Digidesign/Focusrite C24 audio interface/DAW controller.

Some less expensive models come as single PCI cards sporting lots of "professional quality" features. Generally, cards that have analog inputs or outputs and are housed entirely within the computer will have compromised audio quality. Interfaces that can be placed away from the computer and computer monitor screen are less susceptible to picking up noise and hum. These can connect to PCI cards or directly to either the Firewire or

USB ports on the computer. However, for professional-quality multitrack recordings, USB should also be avoided. It simply does not have adequate throughput and is already taxed with both keyboard and mouse duties. (USB 2.0 may be powerful enough for the job, but that remains to be seen.) Interfaces that are connected to PCI cards by long proprietary cables are sometimes referred to as breakout boxes.

Exactly which audio interface is right for a particular job depends on numerous factors:

- **The number of inputs and outputs needed.** How many tracks will you be recording at once? How many channels will you be mixing/monitoring in? How much outboard gear will be used? How many individual outputs will be needed for separate cue mixes?

- **The type of connections needed.** Does the interface need mic preamps? Instrument or line-level analog I/O? What about digital audio connections? MIDI?

- **The software to be used.** Interfaces may or may not be compatible with various software applications.

- **The type of computer to be used.** Mac or PC? Which operating system? Processor and speed? Amount of RAM? Serial busses? Desktop or laptop? Does it have IEEE-1394 or USB? If so, how many ports and which versions?

- **The audio quality desired.** What bit depth and sample rate will you be using? What is the true signal-to-noise ratio of the intended interface? How does the interface address latency issues?

In addition to these basic considerations, many new interfaces offer additional functions once left to other audio devices. These options include:

- Headphone matrix monitoring.

- Format translation.

- ADAT synchronization.

- MIDI machine control.

- Direct injection of instruments.

- Effects processing.

- Analog mixing.

- Equalization.

- Dynamics.

Each of these will be covered in more detail later in this chapter. For now, let's consider the primary function of an interface (after the basic I/O function), which is conversion.

Converters (A/D/A)

Computers deal with digital information only. Anything else must first be converted to binary code for computer processing or storage. In the case of audio, this conversion happens directly from a line-level analog signal. This process is therefore called A/D, short for analog to digital. When analog audio output is desired, the digital data stream must then be reconverted to an analog signal (called D/A).

Quality conversion is essential for accurate, high-fidelity recording. Unfortunately, converters are often overlooked these days, and many manufacturers make misleading claims about performance to boost sales.

Many conversion options are now available, and most digital recording platforms come with converters built in. The prices for the converters alone, however, range widely from as little as $20 to close to $800 per channel. Even more startling is that these converters can appear to have the same functions and quality level, at least on the surface. While factors such as bit depth, sample rate, oversampling, and theoretical signal-to-noise ratios do describe important aspects of the basic function of a converter, they only begin to describe its real quality.

Figure 8.3: Apogee AD16x analog to digital converter.

Below is a breakdown of the basic elements of A/D/A conversion technology.

Analog Elements

One of the most important factors in the quality of any particular converter design is actually the analog circuitry. Good analog components can be expensive, and some manufacturers cut corners in order to decrease cost. Like a steel chain, however, converter quality can only be as strong as its weakest link.

All analog connections should be properly balanced and running at a level of +4dBm. Unbalanced, –10dBV, stereo RCA connections (often labeled "tape in" or "tape out") can be used for flexibility in connecting with consumer audio devices only when necessary. Analog circuits should also be well shielded and properly grounded. A high-quality power supply is critical, as cheaper ones can radiate noise-inducing interference inside the box. External supplies (often called wall warts) are sometimes used to keep noise down. This design compromise alleviates some but not all of these issues.

Every converter design also includes analog filters. As with all analog filters, audible distortion and phase problems can easily occur if the components or design are inferior, or if the filter is too aggressive (and most used in converters are). Again, the better analog filters tend to be pricier.

Sample Rate

The sample rate is the number of times per second a recording system either digitizes incoming sound or converts digital data back to an analog electrical signal. Greater rates translate into the ability to correctly represent higher frequencies. According to the Nyquist Theorem, the highest frequency a system can handle is equal to half its sample rate. The CD standard is 44,100 samples/second (44.1kHz) to adequately represent sound to the upper boundary of human hearing (circa 20kHz). Nothing lower than this rate should be used. Higher rates that are whole-number multiples of 44.1kHz (such as 88.2kHz or 176.4kHz) can be used, but they need to be converted down before standard CDs can be made. The added resolution these high rates offer during the recording, editing, and mixing processes, along with the mathematical simplicity of converting them back down to 44.1kHz, makes the extra storage space and processing power needed worthwhile.

Another popular sample rate is 48kHz, based on a video standard. Use this only if the music you intend to capture will be used as part of a video project; for a CD, it would need to be reconverted to 44.1kHz. This is not only an additional step but can also degrade quality. Many newer systems are also capable of handling rates of 96kHz and 192kHz, both multiples of 48. Recording and working at these rates can be beneficial, but it is not yet clear if the added resolution they offer over the 44.1kHz series outweighs the mathematical inaccuracies of their reconversion for CD.

Bit Depth

As with sample rate, the greater the number of bits used to capture a sound, the more accurately that sound can be represented. Bit depth determines how many values are available to describe the amplitude level of an incoming signal at any given moment. In other words, the number of bits determines the resolution of each sample: the more bits, the greater the resolution. For professional audio purposes, nothing under the 16-bit CD standard should be used; 24-bit systems are now widely available and offer 256 times the resolution of 16. The end result of this increase will be less noisy recordings, even if you do have to convert back down to 16 for printing CDs. Reference your specific software and hardware manuals to determine how to best accomplish 24-bit recording and the subsequent conversion down to 16.

Oversampling

When you convert from analog to digital or vice versa, filters are used to minimize or avoid unwanted byproducts of the conversion process. These filters remove frequencies that are above half the sample rate, which would be misrepresented either as lower tones on input (a process called aliasing) or as high-frequency noise on output. Unfortunately, these filters can cause distortion and phase problems in the audio. Various schemes, designed around temporarily increasing the sample rate, can reduce these problems and/or allow simpler, less expensive filter designs to work more effectively. These processes are called oversampling. Typical rates run anywhere from eight to 128 times faster than the system's base sample rate. Generally speaking, the greater the rate, the better the performance.

Dither

Dither is low-level noise that is purposefully added to a digital audio signal in order to help alleviate, or even mask, some of the limitations of digital recording when representing quieter sounds. As a rule, dither should not be used during multitrack recording. The best time for dither is when creating a final mix and/or when stepping down from 24 to 16 bits (or during any reduction in bit depth). For more specifics on what types of dither are available and when they should be used, refer to the manual of your specific audio software and/or interface.

Word Clock

All digital audio devices are designed to convert and/or output samples at very fast rates. For instance, a standard consumer CD player must read and output almost 85 million bits of data per minute. When two or more devices are linked together digitally, therefore, the smallest discrepancies in their individual sample rates could cause serious audio problems. To combat this, all digital audio transmission formats carry a clocking reference along with the audio data stream. However, when many devices are used and digital signal flow gets even remotely complicated, it is often necessary for all parts of the system to synchronize to a single master clock using a specialized timing signal called word clock. Word clock does not contain audio data or any type of position marker. It is simply a timing reference, making sure each piece of gear moves audio data at the same speed. To simplify and ensure stability, many studios connect all digital gear directly to a special word-clock generator with multiple outputs.

Jitter

Since digital audio information is sent at such high rates, small inconsistencies in timing (called jitter) can cause misrepresentation of samples. This will manifest itself as added noise, loss of clarity, and problems with stereo imaging. Severe jitter can even cause audible popping or clicking in the audio stream. Correct clocking and sync can alleviate this.

Latency & Monitoring

Latency is the time difference between input and output of a digital audio system or signal path. This is caused by algorithmic/mathematical issues as well as purely mechanical/physical procedures and occurs most commonly in software and A/D/A converters and when using hard drives. These time delays can create such problems as: dull or uneven high frequency response, vocals that exhibit a sonically pinched or nasal quality, or a persistent awkwardness on overdubs where musicians can't seem to get the right rhythmic feel, or groove. The latter issue occurs when performers monitor the delayed signal through headphones, or when a mix of input and output is monitored during recording. These situations can cause poor performances or even make accurate playing impossible.

Fortunately, many recording platforms now offer zero latency monitoring. This process simply means that the signal sent to the outputs and/or headphones during recording is split from the input signal before digital conversion (and before it ever enters the computer itself). Be aware, however, that any effects, equalization, or dynamic modifications you may wish to make in the software will not be heard during record monitoring. Also note that since some recording systems allow for both latent and nonlatent signals to be heard simultaneously, you must check with the software and interface manuals to make sure this does not happen.

More expensive, professional, and powerful systems are built to work so fast as to eliminate these performance and monitoring issues. These are often stand-alone systems, which do not rely on a host computer for processing power, or systems that require extra chips added to the computer by way of PCI cards.

Choosing Converters

All the preceding factors in converter design and implementation work together in determining the accuracy and quality of any particular converter, whether stand-alone or integrated into an interface. It is, therefore, important to carefully consider them in choosing a model and integrating it with other studio equipment. Finally, this discussion of A/D/A conversion serves to underscore an important rule of thumb: Once in the digital domain, stay there! Converting back and forth compounds errors, noise, distortion, and phase issues, compromising audio quality each time. With good converters at 24 bits and sample rates of 88.2kHz or higher, this is less of a concern.

Many uninformed or misguided industry professionals (sales reps in particular) claim that the technology of A/D/A conversion has come so far that many inferior designs achieve quite acceptable results. While this may seem true under some conditions (where the monitoring environment is not as accurate or the converter is tested with a stereo program through a single generation of conversion), even small initial differences can have a major impact on the sonic quality of a final product. This is especially true in multitrack recording and mixing environments.

Computers & Software

Compatibility

The platform you select should match the software/hardware combinations that you're looking to implement. Computer models, CPUs, operating systems, audio interfaces, software, and hard drives must all be compatible or the whole system may not run properly. Check intended combinations with audio software and hardware manufacturers before you purchase anything. Sometimes tested and acceptable combinations are updated and posted on manufacturers' Web sites. Complete *turnkey* systems are available from some retailers. These systems usually cost more money but are fully configured, tested, and guaranteed to run smoothly.

CPU Type, Speed & RAM

Especially when you are relying on the computer's CPU to implement real-time audio effects in a multitrack software environment, a faster processing speed and more RAM increases the system's capabilities. With faster processing and a greater amount of RAM, you can use more tracks (a higher track count) and more plug-ins (effects) at one time.

A further note on CPU compatibility: Peripheral audio hardware and software manufacturers sometimes have a difficult time keeping up with the rapid advances, changes, and releases of CPU technology and operating systems. Don't assume that the latest or fastest of either will work the best. Check with all of the manufacturers involved.

In the case of RAM, more is generally better. Most audio recording software allows the user to set a RAM buffer where audio is temporarily stored while recording to, or playing back from, the hard drive. Not infrequently, even fast drives (especially on laptops) experience momentary lag times due to physical jostling, fragmentation, particulate interference, bad sectors, condensation, or recalibration. These short moments can cause clicks or noise in the audio, stop the recording process, or even crash the computer.

The RAM buffer can help with these problems—the bigger the buffer, the more downtime of the hard drive it can handle. There is a trade-off, however, as increasing the buffer also increases lag time (latency). Usually, 256 MB of RAM is a safe minimum for operating only the system and audio software, but again, the more, the better!

Many computer owners use virtual RAM or RAM disks, often without even knowing it. These are designed to supplement the actual installed RAM, but they also slow the system down greatly, and should absolutely not be used for serious audio recording. If you need more RAM, buy it!

Hard Drives

For many computer buyers, hard drives are an afterthought, or they are considered only in terms of capacity. The true performance of a drive's data throughput is actually the most important factor when a professional-level, 24-bit multitrack studio is to be built around it.

One of the most misunderstood factors regarding hard-drive performance is the distinction between the interface speed and the speed of the drive itself. Nowhere is this confusion more evident than in the current hype regarding inexpensive, large-capacity Firewire (IEEE-1394) drives. Firewire is the way the drive interfaces with the computer and does not make the drive fast. It simply means that the interface will probably not be undermining the drive's potential. In many cases, the actual drives built into the cheap Firewire cases are among the slowest on the market. In addition, many manufacturers simply use IDE drives and build an IDE to IEEE-1394 converter inside the case, which diminishes data rates even further. A few companies do make true Firewire drives specifically for audio and video purposes and use great drive mechanisms.

When you are attempting to determine the potential performance of a drive, the interior mechanism is of primary importance. The drive's rotational speed should be fast (7,200 to 10,000 RPMs and above) and its access times low (under 8 milliseconds). Built-in buffers are great for upping the track count but, as always, will create extra lag time. If the drive has fast specs and a small buffer, that's often best. Special A/V drives sometimes offer specialized logic control over the drive's automatic recalibration functions, which is a nice feature. The drive is programmed to wait until recording is over to recalibrate, rather than pausing momentarily to recalibrate in the middle of recording, as many normal drives will do.

Once you've determined that the drive mechanism itself is suitable, consider the interface. On a PC, most drives use the ATA or IDE interfaces. Ultra IDE, Ultra ATA, and Serial

ATA are the fastest of these protocols and can certainly work fine for up to 16 tracks of 16-bit audio at 44.1kHz, especially when used in conjunction with a decent-sized RAM buffer and a fast CPU. With any sizeable increase in track count, bit depth, or sample rate, the drive/interface may be too slow to keep up.

When multiple drives are available, recording "across" the drives, by assigning half of the record tracks to each drive, decreases the burden on the drives and will likely increase the total possible track counts. This approach may also allow you to use a smaller buffer, lowering the system's latency.

Some studios expand on this idea of multiple drives and use what's called a redundant array of independent (or inexpensive) disks (RAID). RAID systems use two or more drives, working in unison, to increase performance and/or fault tolerance by backing up the data. When properly configured, these systems can achieve amazing results.

Interfaces such as SCSI Ultra 2 Wide (80), Ultra 3 (80), Ultra 3 Wide (160), USB 2.0, and IEEE-1394 are also capable of great speeds when used with high-performance drives. USB (1 *or* 2) should generally be avoided, however, as so many other devices are likely to be attached to that bus.

When you are recording simultaneously over 24 tracks in 24 bits, and at sample rates of higher than 48kHz, it is definitely necessary to have lightning-fast A/V drives using specialized RAID arrays or faster interfaces such as IEEE-1394 or SCSI 80/160.

To deliver the best performance, drives should be defragmented (reformatted if possible) before a recording session. This can be done using a number of utility software programs. Also, where possible, one drive should be set aside for all programs, nonsession files, and the operating system only. All audio and session information should be recorded to drives designated only for recording purposes.

Capacity

Multitrack recording requires a lot of drive space. When you are recording in 24 bits at a rate of 44,100 samples per second, one track eats up around 8 MB/minute. With 24 tracks, that means 192 MB/minute or a total 672 MB for the average song. Recording a 42-minute, 12-song album at this rate would take over 8 gigabytes of drive space. At the higher audio quality of 24 bits/96 kHz, the same album would require around 18 GB. Furthermore, with normal working methods including mixes, overdubs, comp tracks, effects files, and session files, these figures increase significantly. Depending on studio workload, a 200 GB drive could be filled in a couple of weeks! The moral of the story: You cannot have too much drive space.

Backup

Often the best way to back up sessions is to create either a CD-R or DVD-R data archive of the entire project as soon as it's over. The best situation is for the studio computer to have both a fast CD/DVD player and a fast DVD-R/CD-R. This way you can also make copies quickly. The clients should be supplied with backups, and copies should also remain in the studio archive.

Peripheral Busses

Most PCs still come with serial and PS/2 ports for attaching keyboards, mice, writing tablets, and joysticks as well as parallel ports for printers and scanners. Since Macintosh machines began relying on the more powerful USB and IEEE-1394 interfaces, those have now found their way into many PCs as well. For connecting professional audio devices, USB and IEEE-1394 ports are a must. Look for a computer with three of four of each.

Expansion Capabilities

Many audio and MIDI interfaces, along with other recording devices, rely on expansion slots to connect with the computer. Specially designed cards are added by way of either PCI or PCMCIA slots. Depending on the exact nature of the hardware to be used, a studio computer may require three or more free slots.

Additional concerns revolve around planning for the future. As software and operating systems evolve they usually require a greater amount of RAM and a faster processor. Can these be easily upgraded in your computer, or will you need to buy another one?

Fans & Monitors

Two other important factors for a studio computer are the fan and the monitor. The fan should be extra quiet and reliable. No noise should be heard in the control room to disturb either listening or recording.

Since multitrack recording software relies on so many windows to perform various tasks, either a large computer monitor or an array of two or more is a necessity in the studio.

Audio Software

Currently there are over a dozen professional-level computer applications dedicated to the recording and editing of digital audio and MIDI. While the basic functionality is similar, the specific implementation and user interfaces vary significantly. When choosing a program consider the following questions:

- Does it run on Macintosh, PC, or both?

- Does it require a specific version of the operating system?

- What are its minimum CPU and RAM requirements?

- How many audio tracks does it support (and how many do you need)?

- Which audio interfaces are compatible?

- What bit depths and sample rates are supported?

- Does the graphic interface feel intuitive to you?

Figure 8.4: Pro Tools® DAW software by Digidesign®.

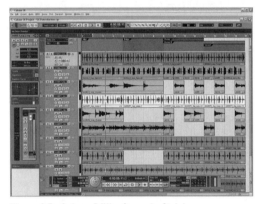

Figure 8.5: Cubase DAW software by Steinberg.

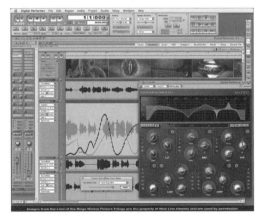

Figure 8.6: Digital Performer DAW software by Mark of the Unicorn.

Larger local music stores may be able to help you answer these questions and give demonstrations of several competing programs. Here are the titles and publishers of the major multitrack recording/editing programs currently available:

- Pro Tools®, Digidesign®
- Digital Performer, Mark of the Unicorn
- AudioDesk, Mark of the Unicorn
- Deck, BIAS
- Nuendo, Steinberg
- Cubase, Steinberg
- Sonar, Cakewalk
- Unity Session, BitHeadz
- Logic, Apple Computer (Emagic)
- Cool Edit Pro, Syntrillium
- Paris, URS Digital

File Structure

A number of audio applications generate multiple types of computer files. The main document created is often merely a description of exactly how to play a series of separate audio files. Depending on the software, this main document might be called any number of things: for example, session, project, sequence, or edit decision list (EDL). Some programs also save effects and cross-fades separately.

All of these files need to be kept together and well organized. Most audio applications do this automatically, but you should be aware of how your software deals with these issues for times when you're working outside the software or when there are exceptions to its general organizational scheme, which there inevitably are.

File Formats

When audio is written to a computer hard drive through a software application, it can be stored in numerous formats depending on operating system, software manufacturer, and delivery method (Web, CD, video clip, etc.). The most common high-quality formats are WAV, AIF, and SDII. Use WAV on computers running Windows, SDII if you're running the Pro Tools software. AIF is often used as a generic format that can be read by a majority of systems, but unfortunately, it is not always the best format. Read the software manuals to know which format a particular application favors.

Web-based formats (such as MP3) should never be used as the original capture or storage format, because they compromise quality to various degrees in order to reduce file sizes. If Web delivery is ultimately desired, create a second copy in the appropriate format. Always keep the high-quality original WAV, AIF, or SDII files archived and unchanged.

Editing

Most audio programs display sound as a waveform of amplitude over time, and include both positive and negative portions of the cycle. These curves can be edited easily using techniques and tools similar to those of word processing. Simple functions such as cut, copy, and paste are merged with the musical building blocks of volume, time, and even space (in most cases, stereo).

All edits are either destructive or nondestructive. A destructive edit is one in which the sound file is changed or rewritten. Nondestructive edits simply create descriptions of how to modify the audio and then perform these during playback; the actual audio file on disk is not changed. Nondestructive editing is processor and RAM intensive but does not take up extra hard drive space.

Whenever possible, use nondestructive editing. Since it leaves the original files intact, you can undo any changes. The actual undo command in most software can be quite helpful, but don't rely on it as a safety function for destructive editing.

Drivers

Each device added to or connected to the computer need a small software program to integrate it with the operating system and audio software. These programs are called drivers (extensions in Mac land). While some manufacturers rely on the generic drivers built into the operating system, others prefer the extra flexibility and power they get by writing their own. Make sure these drivers are up to date and installed properly, and work with your specific operating system. Again, check with the hardware and software manufacturers for the latest information on drivers and compatibility.

Microphones

When you are recording from acoustic sources, the microphone may be the single most important part of the signal path. It is responsible for changing sound energy from an acoustical state to an electrical one. The specific way in which a microphone completes this change (or transduction) of energy affects the quality or color of the sound and the way in which it is represented through the rest of the recording process. It is therefore important to

Figure 8.7: Sennheiser e602 large-diaphragm dynamic microphone.

Figure 8.8: Blue Microphones' the Mouse, a large-diaphragm condenser mic.

have a varied collection of microphones and to select the right one for each recording task. Decisions concerning which microphones to use under which conditions require knowing about the different types and specifications available. Let's start with the basic types of transducers.

Dynamic

Like speakers, dynamic microphones function on the principle of electromagnetic induction, only in reverse. A diaphragm captures vibrations in the air and translates them into its own mechanical movement. A coil of wire, attached to the back of the diaphragm, oscillates within a magnetic field, creating an electrical signal similar to the movement of the diaphragm, and therefore the original sound.

Because of their simple construction and operating principles, dynamic microphones are not only robust and reliable but also tend to be less expensive than other types (circa $15–$450). But generally speaking, they are not the most sonically accurate of microphone types.

Ribbon

Ribbon microphones also work on an electromagnetic induction design. In this case, a thin metal ribbon is suspended in a magnetic field. When the ribbon vibrates in response to sound, an electric signal is generated through the ribbon (which therefore acts as a combination of diaphragm and electrical inducer).

These microphones are generally quite accurate and are known for exhibiting a warm and desirable tone. Due to their design, many ribbons require more amplification (gain) than other microphone types and are more expensive than dynamics (circa $500–$3,000). Though traditional designs are also quite fragile, breakthroughs using modern materials have made some of the newer models much more rugged.

Condenser

Condenser, or capacitor, microphones transduce acoustical energy into electrical energy by creating changes in capacitance as a charged diaphragm vibrates, varying its proximity to an equally charged back plate. When the capacitance changes, the voltage responds both inversely and proportionately. This design requires a power source to operate the microphone, usually supplied from a microphone preamplifier by way of phantom power (see the preamplifier section).

While high-quality traditional condenser mics tend to be expensive (circa $500–$6,000), recent designs and manufacturing techniques have created a wide range of inexpensive models as well (circa $150–$600).

These low-priced microphones can sound very good, but keep in mind that the price break usually comes with a reduction in a model's options and/or the use of lower-quality components and looser manufacturing tolerances. These microphones may not have the longevity or consistency of more expensive models.

Another recent development in condenser design is the invention of the electret. The diaphragm or back plate of an electret condenser is made from a new material that stores a static charge permanently and therefore requires less power to operate. Although an external power supply is not necessary, these microphones usually run on a small battery that can often be used for thousands of hours before it needs replacing. Some sound engineers, not even aware that these microphones have batteries, take them in for service when they stop working after many years of use. Phantom power from the preamplifier can also be used on these microphones to extend battery life. Due in part to simpler circuitry, electrets tend to be much less expensive than traditional condensers.

The nature of the condenser design allows for a wide and even frequency response. Units can even be miniaturized, with capsules ranging in size from mere millimeters to three or more centimeters. Though some newer models are pretty hardy, condensers should generally be considered fragile.

Figure 8.9: Audio-Technica 4041 small-diaphragm condenser mic.

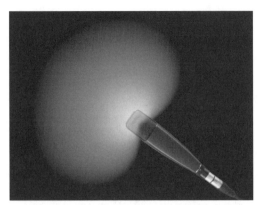

Figure 8.10: Cardioid mic pattern, Sennheiser MD421.

Figure 8.11: Figure-eight mic pattern, Sennheiser MKH30.

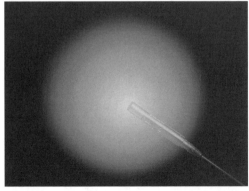

Figure 8.12: Omnidirectional mic pattern, Sennheiser MKH20.

Polar Patterns

Microphone polar patterns refer to the microphone's relative sensitivity at various angles in a 360-degree circle around the capsule. The zero-degree reference runs perpendicular to the front of the diaphragm. Sound waves hitting the microphone from that angle are said to be on-axis. Pictograms are often used to represent the five most common patterns.

Cardioid (unidirectional) Most sensitive to sound coming at the front, least sensitive from the rear.

Cardioid patterns are useful for helping to isolate the sound from one particular instrument or direction. For example, a cardioid microphone on the snare of a full drum kit can be angled to be most sensitive to the snare and least sensitive to the toms or hi-hat.

Bidirectional (figure-eight) Most sensitive to sound from 0 degrees, on-axis with the front of the diaphragm as well as at 180 degrees (to the rear of the diaphragm). Least sensitive in between (at 90 and 270 degrees).

Bidirectional mics are great for picking up a blend of two singers facing each other, while rejecting sound from the sides. They are often used to pick up both direct and reflected sound.

Omnidirectional Equal sensitivity in all directions.

An omnidirectional mic is used to get the best sense of the acoustic environment. Also, since it tends to have the most accurate frequency response of the patterns, it is often used for scientific measurements and full-frequency classical recordings.

Supercardioid Similar to cardioid, except it has some sensitivity to the rear and rejects sound most from 120 degrees and 240 degrees off axis.

Hypercardioid Similar to bidirectional, except it has slightly less sensitivity to the rear and rejects sound most from 105 degrees and 255 degrees off axis.

Proximity Effect

Directional microphones tend to emphasize low frequencies more when the mic is placed closer to the sound source. This is known as proximity effect. Equalization can be used to offset this effect, usually in the form of a highpass filter or a negative-gain low shelf. Some microphones have highpass filters built in to combat this effect as well as general low-end rumble. Of course this filtering can be done in other places, such as the preamp, mixing board, or software.

Sensitivity

Sensitivity is a measurement of a microphone's output voltage when exposed to a given standardized input. The greater the output, the less amplification the signal will need to reach line level. Because less gain is required, less noise is added to the signal.

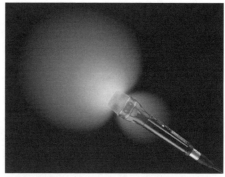

Figure 8.13: Supercardioid mic pattern, Sennheiser MD431.

Frequency Response

The relative sensitivity of a microphone to various frequencies across the audible range is described as its frequency response. This is often charted on a graph, which compares the average output level of the microphone being tested to the output level of frequencies throughout the range. These measurements may be given at various distances from, or angles to, the microphone diaphragm. If no angle is specified, assume that the measurements are for the response from the angle of greatest sensitivity (0 degrees).

Figure 8.14: Hypercardioid mic pattern, Sennheiser MKH70.

The particular frequency response characteristics of a microphone make its sonic color distinct from other mics. Sometimes microphone specs include a greatly simplified version of this information, stating an effective frequency range in which the microphone stays within a certain sensitivity variance (for example, 30–15,000Hz ± 3dB).

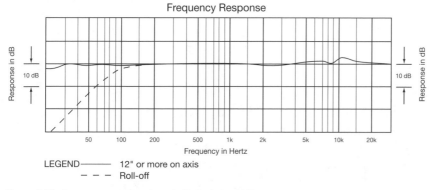

Figure 8.15: Frequency response chart, Audio-Technica 4041.

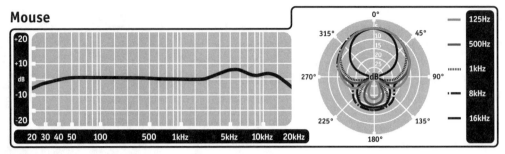

Figure 8.16: Frequency response chart, Blue Microphones' the Mouse.

Off-Axis Coloration

Off-axis coloration refers to the way in which the frequency response of a microphone varies depending on the sound's relative angle to the diaphragm. This can be compared to the response on-axis (0 degrees) to describe the coloration effect.

Transient Response

The transient response measures how quickly the diaphragm of a microphone can react to a change in sound pressure. This is directly related to the mass of the diaphragm and its consequent inertia, and it greatly affects a microphone's character. To capture sounds with a strong, aggressive attack, you need a microphone with a fast response. On the other hand, a slower transient response helps tame these kinds of sounds, if desired.

Equivalent Noise

The amount of noise the microphone itself generates is known as its equivalent noise. This is expressed as the amount of dB (SPL) that would produce an output voltage equivalent to the level of the microphone's self-noise. Obviously, less is better.

SPL Handling

This refers to the maximum sound pressure level (in dB) a microphone can be subjected to before it distorts due to overload. You should take these ratings seriously, as you can damage some microphones when subjecting them to sound pressures beyond this maximum level. If you are not yet familiar with relative SPLs, you can determine them with measuring devices, as discussed in chapter 2.

Impedance (Z)

Impedance is the measure of a microphone's electrical resistance (in ohms). This can have an effect on the amount of noise a mic picks up over longer cable runs, as well as its output level and the way in which it interacts with the preamplifier.

Polarity

Polarity refers to the way in which positive and negative sides of the electrical signal are treated. The electrical convention for balanced audio, especially in the U.S., is that pin two is positive (or hot) and three is negative (or cold). Unfortunately some older equipment, as well as some European gear, reverses this. It is also not uncommon to find cabling and connectors that have been assembled, often inadvertently, with pin three positive. If any studio equipment is wired this way, it should be switched back. You can use special polarity-inverting connectors to bring it back to pin two positive.

Stereo Microphones

There are numerous stereo microphones on the market today. These are specialty microphones with two separate diaphragm elements, angled in such a manner as to pick up from two distinct directions. These can be useful for overhead drum miking as well as live recordings or any other situation in which a coherent stereo image is desired.

For ease of use and consistency in quality of the stereo signal, an XY (coincident) electret condenser microphone is a good choice. This type is really two unidirectional microphones in one, often designed to pick up sound in a 90-degree fashion: The left element is most sensitive to sound from 45 degrees left of center, and the right element is most sensitive to sound from 45 degrees right of center. Other common angles range up to 120 degrees.

MS (mid-side) or binaural stereo microphones can also be used and are capable of making superb recordings. With these mics you must take greater care, however, in placement, settings, panning, mixing, and cabling.

Microphone Pairs

You can also achieve a stereo recording with a pair of mono microphones. To facilitate this, some manufacturers offer models in matched pairs, which means that they have gone to great lengths to ensure that the performance of the two mics is as close to identical as possible.

Sometimes pairs of microphones are sold with consecutive serial numbers. While these are not guaranteed to be as similar as matched pairs, the idea is that their components likely came from the same stock, and similar manufacturing procedures and conditions were used to assemble them.

Microphone Kits

Numerous manufacturers and equipment retailers offer prepackaged sets of microphones, often at a discount. Usually, these collections are tailored for particular uses, such as live sound reinforcement, drum sets, stereo recording, or surround sound. A good kit can be a cost-effective way to quickly improve a studio's microphone selection. The only drawback is that they tend to limit selection to a single manufacturer. With the money saved, however, you could purchase additional microphones to expand recording options.

Figure 8.17: Drum microphone kit by Audio-Technica.

Accessories

Microphones for use outdoors, or in any sort of air current, should be equipped with a windscreen to keep moving air from blowing on the microphone element, causing a rumble in the recording. Some microphones come with foam filters that fit around the capsule, but after-market versions are also available.

Pop filters (plosive filters) work on a similar concept. These are generally made of a fine mesh material (like pantyhose) stretched inside a round hoop. The hoop is held in front of a microphone by either a gooseneck or rigid boom arm. The pop filter blocks moving air from the singer's mouth from hitting the mic element, but lets the sound through.

A shock mount is also a good idea, as it helps isolate the mic from any ground, floor, or stand vibrations that could generate unwanted noises in the recording. Different models of microphones are more and less sensitive to these types of mechanical vibrations. Some are even internally suspended in a shock mount. A bass roll-off (high pass) filter, often included on the microphone, may also address these issues. Be aware, however, that filtering also permanently removes all low frequencies from the recording, not just unwanted "rumbles."

Microphone Preamplifiers

Most microphones produce signals that are too weak for recording directly. An amplifier, known as a microphone preamplifier (or mic pre), must be used to bring the signal up to a more appropriate level. Complicating this process further is the fact that both voltage and electrical resistance, called impedance, can vary greatly from one microphone to the next. Mic pres must be able to handle a wide range of level and impedance in order to deliver standard line-level signals without degrading the quality of the audio.

Figure 8.18: Summit 2BA-221 microphone preamplifier.

Preamplifiers are found in some audio interfaces, mixing consoles, and stand-alone recording platforms. They can also be purchased separately to allow for greater flexibility of system configuration. As with microphones themselves, different preamp designs impart their own sonic personalities to the input material. An array of quality microphone preamps allows greater flexibility in the sonic character of a studio.

Generally speaking, microphone preamplifiers are designed for either accuracy or personality. In the first case, the manufacturer uses the highest quality components and takes great care in all aspects of the circuit design to create a device with a flat frequency response and low distortion throughout its gain range. The goal is to change the character of the sound source as little as possible. These designs can be very expensive. Preamps that fall under the personality category can be just as useful and are sometimes just as costly. They are designed to impart a particular sonic character, which may change as the gain is increased. Some of these preamps have the ability to vary the impedance. This has an interactive effect with the microphone that varies the level, frequency response, and coloration achieved.

Figure 8.19: Apogee Mini MP microphone preamplifier.

A rotary knob (called a pot) adjusts the level of amplification (gain or trim) an incoming microphone signal receives. The amount of amplification controlled by this knob is often split into two ranges using a switch called a pad. When activated, an average pad *decreases* the amount of amplification by 12 to 26dB. This function is necessary because of the enormous range of voltages output by microphones.

As mentioned in the microphone section, some mics require electrical current to operate. This can be supplied by battery, in the case of electret mics, or by a 48-volt current sent from the mic preamp. The latter is called phantom power and is necessary for most traditional condenser designs. Preamps usually have a switch to turn phantom on or off, but some consoles offer no such control—if the mixer is on, so is phantom power. This can be hazardous to some mics, as a power spike can surge through the phantom supply when a mic is either plugged into or unplugged from a hot phantom source. You should always switch off phantom power when connecting or disconnecting microphones.

Other options on mic pres include phase switches and highpass filters. Activating the phase switch inverts the signal's phase by 180 degrees. In the analog realm, this is done by switching negative and positive electrical leads. A phase switch can be used to match the phase of mismatched gear or cabling, and it is also often used to combat interference issues between two or more microphones (more on this in chapter 14).

A highpass filter (HPF, sometimes called a low-cut filter) is designed to allow frequencies above a user-defined point to pass through. All lower frequencies are stripped out of the audio. These filters are used to remove the low-frequency resonances of some rooms, air-conditioning, wind noise, plosives, proximity effect, and mechanical vibrations passed through the mic stand.

Good metering is also important when you are using a microphone preamp. For ease of use, and to ensure the best signal-to-noise ratio, preamps should have attached input and output meters to show levels. Moving needle displays (called VUs) and multiple LEDs are common ways to graphically represent the relative strength of an audio signal. Generally speaking, the more values these meters can represent, the better. A peak indicator may also be included and is useful for determining if a signal has gone above the distortion threshold.

Mixers

A mixer (a.k.a. console, board, or desk) is a device that controls how multiple audio inputs are routed, modified, mixed together, and sent back out in real time. Mixers come in many configurations for studio recording, live sound reinforcement, radio, and video/film post-production. Consoles are also available with a wide array of features in either the analog or digital realms, and can be either hardware or software based (sometimes both). Be aware that while software mixers can be just as powerful as hardware ones, they do not have the same visual impact on potential or current clients checking out the control room. You can compensate for this somewhat with other visually alluring studio elements or a mixing control surface (discussed in more detail later in this chapter). While still striking in appearance, a mixing control surface does not have the high price tag of a traditional pro-quality desk.

Figure 8.20: Mackie 3Z•8 analog console.

Since mixers now come in so many configurations, many of them open-ended and user-configurable, let's take a look at some of their basic functions.

Channels

A channel is an individual signal-input pathway into the mixer. It can have many options for modifying or routing that signal, including:

- *Microphone preamplifier* (input): Used to connect mics and amplify their signals. The preamp section can also include phase invert switching, a highpass filter, a pad, and phantom power. (For a more thorough discussion of preamps, see the section earlier in this chapter.)

- *Line input:* A dedicated input for line-level signals (generally from –10dBV to +4dBm) that don't require as much amplification as mic signals.

- *Hi-Z input* (instrument input): A dedicated input for the higher impedance of many electric instruments.

- *Insert:* Both an output and input from the channel. Inserts are generally used to send the signal through an effect, EQ, or dynamics processor and then return it to the channel. The insert can also be used to get signal to and from a tape machine, monitor mixer, or anywhere else you might need it.

- *Direct out:* Sends signal from a single channel out of the mixer, usually to a multitrack recorder. Direct outs may or may not have level controls.

- *Auxiliary send:* Used to send signal out of one or more channels, often to an effects unit or to create separate mixes. Auxiliary sends come with a knob (sometimes a slider) to control level and can be either pre- or postchannel fader. Sends that are prefader are not affected by the level of the main channel fader. If the main fader is down but the prefader aux is up, then the signal will not go to the main stereo mix but can still get to an external effects unit (or wherever). When an aux send is postfader, its output level is scaled by the main channel fader. When the channel level is brought down, so is the amount sent from the aux.

- *Tape return:* A secondary input that acts independently of the channel strip signal path. It is designed to give control of the signal after it returns from being recorded to a multitrack. When recording, you might use the channel faders to control the amount of signal sent to the multitrack, while the tape returns create a stereo mix of the audio coming back from the tape. The considerations regarding good levels for recording and mixing are not the same, so this way you can control them separately. When tracking (recording) is done, some consoles allow you to flip these two functions so that the tape return signal can make use of the primary faders, EQ, dynamics, and aux sends. Sometimes the tape return signal path is merely a small fader or knob for level control, and a pan pot.

Figure 8.21: Tascam DM-3200 digital console.

- *Equalization* (EQ): Allows frequency-specific boosting or cutting of the audio. Can be used to change the tonal character of the sound or to remove problem frequency areas. EQ is very important, so the more bands, the better. They should also be highly flexible in terms of both control and function (more on EQ later in this chapter).

- *Dynamics:* Allow the user to make automatic level adjustments (see separate section later in this chapter).

- *Fader* (channel): A large slider at the bottom of the channel strip used to adjust the level (amount) of the audio signal.

- *Panning:* Adjusts the amount of signal being sent relative to two or more busses. Panning can be used to control a signal's placement within the stereo or surround fields. You control relative level by a rotary knob, horizontal (x-axis) slider, joystick, XY screen matrix, or a combination of these.

- *Bus:* A shared signal path accessible by many channels. A single bus goes to a single location (either within the mixer or to an output), but the signal can come from multiple channels. Busses can be used to send signals to the stereo master fader, surround master, subgroups, tape (called track assign), or bus outputs. (Aux sends are also a form of bus.)

- *Solo:* When activated, solo sends that specific channel to the monitors while temporarily muting nonsoloed channels. There are many versions of solo, however, so read the manual to determine exactly how a particular console functions. It may be pre- or post-fader and may or may not affect particular outputs, including the tape outs. In some instances a solo only affects what you hear in the headphones and not the master stereo bus! Find out before pressing a solo button while recording something.

- *Mute:* Sometimes indicated as just on/off, mute stops the signal from that channel from getting to any postfader busses or auxes. Beware, however, and read the manual to determine how it affects prefader sends, inserts, or direct outs.

Master Section

The master section is a part of the mixer to which channels and other signals are bussed. It includes control of the levels of groups of channels, effects returns, and the amount of the overall master mix, sent to "tape" (or other mixdown media) as well as to the various monitoring options. The master section can also house controls that modify or define the function of the board as a whole. Some of the common parameters are:

- *Subgroup* (submaster or group): A fader to which the signal can be bussed and combined from multiple channels. In the mixing process, subgroups make it easier to control the level of a group of instruments. All of the drum kit microphones, for instance, could be mixed and panned relative to each other using the channel faders and then bussed to a stereo subgroup. The subgroup is, in turn, bussed to the final master fader. This way, if you decide to bring the drums down a bit in the mix to make way for the vocals, all you need to do is pull down one fader rather than 16!

- *Auxiliary return* (aux or effects return): An input into the master section of the console for adding effects back into the overall mix. These effects, it is assumed, were originally sent from the individual input channels by way of the aux sends.

- *Master fader:* A single control (usually a big red slider) that affects the overall level of the final mix.

- *Monitoring:* There are often many knobs used to control the signal level from the master fader going to various places. They can control monitoring levels for various rooms and speaker systems as well as for the engineer's headphones.

- *Solo:* An optional master-level control for soloed channels and an assignment for exactly where the signal is sent and in what mode the solo is functioning. Be aware that if the solo master level is turned way up, activating a channel solo button can actually *increase* the volume of the audio to the monitors.

- *Two-track out* (tape out): A single control to adjust the level of the final mix being sent to a master recorder.

- *Two-track in* (tape in): A special stereo (now sometimes surround) input level control that accepts a final master mix input back from the master recorder and sends it to the various monitoring outputs. This lets you hear what the final product sounds like after the mix is complete.

- *Talkback:* Controls the level going from a special control room mic back to the performers' headphone mixes. Talkback allows the engineer to communicate with performers even though they are in different rooms.

Figure 8.22: Tascam 2400 DAW controller.

Metering

Professional consoles should be equipped to display the levels of all channel inputs (prefader for tracking) as well as postfader channel levels (for mixing). Proper level settings are extremely important during recording, mixing, and mastering. Audio quality can easily be compromised if incorrect levels are used at any stage in the process. Levels that are too low at some point in the chain cause excessive noise, while levels that are too high cause distortion. Therefore, thorough and accurate metering is essential. Digital consoles should show both RMS (average) and peak levels. They should also indicate when the signal has gone above maximum level (causing distortion). Master outputs and groups must also have good meters.

Other Features

- *Scene memory:* Captures where all of the mixer's functions are set at a given moment so you can recall them later. Most digital, hardware mixers have this now and so do some expensive analog models. Almost all software platforms have this capability built in.

- *Automation:* The ability for a mixer to record, edit, and play back real-time continuous changes in the positions and settings of all its various parameters. Only the more expensive analog hardware consoles have automation with built-in memory and control. Many less expensive digital boards can do automation if controlled from a computer or other external device, and almost all software platforms have this capability built in.

- *Internal effects:* Many mixers now come equipped with integrated internal effects processors. These vary greatly in size, scope, and power.

Overall Concerns

Since mixing consoles are a fundamental part of the recording studio, the following factors should be kept in mind when choosing one.

- *Sound quality:* Consider factors such as the signal-to-noise ratio, frequency response, and any tonal coloration the board adds to the sound.

- *Power:* Be sure the console has what you need as far as the number of input channels, outputs, busses, panning (stereo versus surround), groups, EQ, dynamics, interfacing, built-in effects, etc.

- *Flexibility:* Can the board be easily assigned to do different functions, changing its signal routing and work mode?

- *Ease of use:* Are things displayed in a manner that makes their functions clear? Is it all labeled well?

- *Ergonomics:* Can you get to each of the functions you need during a normal session quickly and easily? If not, sessions will be slowed down and everyone will become frustrated.

- *Visual appeal:* Does the mixer have the "wow" factor? Does it call attention to itself and instill an excitement in the clients? (You do want those, don't you?)

Monitoring

Accurate monitoring is often practically overlooked when it comes to the design and implementation of many facilities, especially project studios. Because the recording and mixing engineers working in these studios do not hear an accurate balance of sonic elements, they are often led to make inappropriate decisions. Due to this handicap, their final product may consistently translate poorly onto other playback systems, which can quickly ruin the reputation of both the studio and the engineers.

Good monitoring in the control room requires an accurate acoustic environment (see chapter 7), high-quality monitor speakers, correct speaker placement, appropriate amplifiers, calibrated crossovers, professional headphones, master EQ, and careful attention to levels.

Larger professional studios often have big monitor speakers placed back into the front wall so that the speakers are flush with the wall itself. These setups offer great bass response (due to the infinite baffle created by being flush with the wall) and a wide useful listening space, but are quite expensive and difficult to install. A less costly approach is to place a pair of smaller speakers (known as near-fields) close to the main listening position. This proximity tends to minimize the acoustic effects of the room and enhance stereo imaging. At the same time, the best listening position, sometimes called the sweet spot, becomes very small. If the engineer moves, even by a foot or so, the accuracy of both frequency response and imaging can be severely compromised.

Figure 8.23: Alesis M1 Active near-field studio monitors.

To extend the usable bass response of near-field monitors, you can use a subwoofer. This should be carefully selected and matched to the near-fields, which is most easily done if you purchase a matched set from a single manufacturer. To ensure there's no accentuation of the frequencies being covered by both speaker types, specialized filters (called crossovers) are used. Crossovers must be carefully set, as should the relative level between the sub and the stereo pair.

In recent years more and more studios have been gearing up to record and mix in surround. While there are numerous surround configurations, the most common is known as 5.1, which signifies that there are five full-range channels/speakers and one low-frequency channel/subwoofer. Because of variations in the nature and performance of the subwoofer, you must use a method called bass management to configure the system's performance. Bass management determines whether the lower frequencies of the full-range channels will be sent to the sub only, to both the full-range and sub, or to just the full-range speakers. In the last case, only the audio already dedicated to the .1 LFE (low-frequency effects) channel is sent to the subwoofer. Obviously, the use of surround monitoring systems requires a well-matched speaker system and careful acoustic planning.

Regardless of whether a studio setup is in stereo or surround, the main monitoring speakers should be of the highest quality and intended for professional studio use. Speakers intended for the home theater, hi-fi, DJ, automotive, or live sound markets should not be used as substitutes. These are often designed to "enhance" the sound in some way by modifying frequency response and/or phase. At the same time, however, it is a good idea to have a second pair of lower quality home or computer speakers on which to check final mixes. After all, a final mix released on CD might be played on a fantastic audiophile system *or* on a computer or cheap boom box.

Another factor to consider when choosing a monitoring system is the desired working and maximum SPL (loudness). A main studio monitoring system should be capable of reaching and sustaining high volumes (around 110dB SPL at listening position) without distorting or damaging any components. With most near-fields, this requires at least 120–150 watts of power from the amplifier. To be safe, the speakers themselves should be rated to handle between 150 to 200 percent of this figure in either RMS (average) or sustained power. Momentary power spikes, called peaks, may be even higher, so speakers also come with peak power ratings. These should be at least double the high end of the operating RMS power range.

Amplifiers are rated to deliver different amounts of power based on the attached speakers' electrical resistance. With most studio speakers, this ranges through 16, 8, and 4 ohms. The lower the impedance of the speaker, the more power the amp will deliver. At the same time, take care not to expose the amp to either too much or too little resistance. This can cause it (and the speakers) harm. Be sure to match components to keep impedances within recommended operating ranges. Read the speaker and amplifier manuals to help configure the system.

Once your system is installed and configured, configure the amplifiers and/or mixer monitor outputs so that they will not exceed your predetermined maximum power rating. Also note that while people should not expose themselves to these types of levels for very long (see chapter 14), many bands and solo artists will want to hear final mixes at high volumes. Audio engineers should be prepared to accommodate them with the proper amplifier/speaker combinations and a good set of personal earplugs.

The process of matching amplifiers and speakers is quickly becoming a thing of the past, however, in near-field monitoring. More and more models now come powered, with the amplifiers and crossovers built right in. The benefits are numerous: The components are well matched and appropriate, and issues of power, impedance, and crossovers are addressed by the manufacturer. The only drawback of powered speakers is that they tend to be both heavy and hot.

The frequency response of studio monitors should be relatively flat from the low end (around 20 to 60Hz) all the way up past 18kHz at least. In many current high-quality professional models, responses within this range vary less than ±1.5dB. The smaller this number, the better.

Figure 8.24: Sennheiser HD280 closed-back headphones.

Headphones

In the studio, performers use headphones when tracking, and so does the engineer when recording and mixing. The best type of headphones to use depends on the task.

Headphones for the control room should completely enclose each ear and be highly accurate. They should color the sound as little as possible so that the engineer can get the best picture of what the mix really sounds like. These headphones can be expensive (around $85–$350), but only a few pairs are needed.

Any headphones used by musicians during the recording process should be rugged! If the instrument being recorded is very loud, such as drums or electric guitar, either closed- or open-backed models can be used. The primary concerns (after durability) should be impedance and maximum SPL. Since the headphones must be loud to compete with the instrument itself, look for a high maximum SPL rating and low impedance, along with a powerful amplifier (more on that below).

If the instrument being recorded is not that loud, and the headphones are close to the microphone, a closed-back design should be used to minimize sound escaping and feeding back into the microphone.

All headphones should be comfortable and adjustable for fit.

Cue Mixers & Amplifiers

In order to power all of the headphones used during a tracking session (often six or more pairs), studios need special headphone amplifiers. Because what the performers hear while tracking affects their comfort and inspiration, many studios also allow a separate mix (called a cue mix) for each performer. Some systems even make provisions for the performers to create their own mixes. Though cue mixers and individual cue mixers are pricier than passive amps, they are well worth the expense.

Equalizers

Equalizers are used to either accentuate (boost) or attenuate (cut) frequencies within a specified range. EQ can be used to address frequency-specific audio problems or clear up a mix by stressing the more necessary ranges of individual instruments or vocals. Whether software or hardware based, professional-quality EQ is an essential part of any studio.

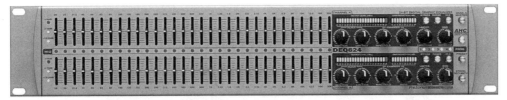

Figure 8.25: PreSonus DEQ624 graphic equalizer.

Figure 8.26: TL Audio Ivory 2 – 5013 parametric equalizer.

Less-expensive consumer units can introduce noise and phase problems into the audio. There are many types of EQ, four of which are most popular in studios:

- *Highpass:* Removes audio below a certain cutoff frequency, allowing the higher frequencies to pass unaltered. Controls may include cutoff frequency and slope.

- *Lowpass:* Removes audio above a certain cutoff frequency, allowing the lower frequencies to pass unaltered. Controls may include cutoff frequency and slope.

- *Shelving* (high and low): A high shelf either boosts or cuts all audio above a certain cutoff frequency. A low shelf either boosts or cuts all audio below a certain cutoff frequency. Controls generally include frequency and amount.

- *Notch* (or peaking): Boosts or cuts a frequency range in a certain response curve around a center frequency. The size of the affected range is called the bandwidth, described in hertz, and is determined by the Q (short for quality factor) of the EQ circuit. Q is a measure of how sharp the shape of the peak is. A higher Q means a smaller bandwidth, and a lower Q means a greater bandwidth. EQ units include controls for bandwidth (or Q) as well as for center frequency and amount. When all three of these factors are user definable, notch filters are referred to as fully parametric. A series of notch filters controlled by a bank of individual faders is called a graphic EQ. Both center frequencies and Q are often fixed on graphic EQ units, which are prized not for their flexibility but ease of use.

Figure 8.27: Universal Audio Pultec EQP-1A parametric equalizer plug-in.

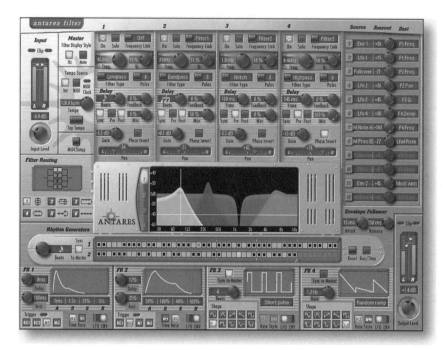

Figure 8.28: Antares Filter equalizer plug-in.

Effects

All studios need a wide array of effects available to make exciting and professional-sounding recordings. Effects come in both hardware and software versions. While software is much less expensive and offers a wider array of effects, dedicated hardware units can be more powerful, yet don't tax the CPU (taking away from track counts) or crash the system!

To alleviate demands on the computer's CPU, some manufacturers offer secondary processors that can be added to the computer through expansion slots or other busses (generally IEEE-1394). These additional DSP (digital signal processing) chips are dedicated to computing audio effects. Systems utilizing DSP technology generally have greater track counts and effects power along with lower latency. Software effects themselves are either destructive or nondestructive (see the section above on audio software).

The following are just some of the effects commonly used in the studio:

- *Delay:* Simply, delay holds an incoming audio signal for a short amount of time before sending it out, and is a basic element of numerous other effects. Short delays can be used to produce distinctive comb filtering, doubling, chorus, or flanging effects. Longer delays are used to create the effects of reverb and echo. Studios should have many types of delay effects available simultaneously.

- *Reverb:* The emulation of an acoustic environment through multiple delays and EQ. Reverb lends a recording its sense of space. Though there are settings that create a "natural" reverb effect, reverb processors can also create virtual spaces that cannot exist in the real world. Studios should have several high-quality reverbs. It is not necessary to have one instance per track because reverbs are often shared on a single auxiliary send of the mixer.

- *Chorus:* An effect that uses a continually varying delay time and pitch shifting to achieve the sound of multiple performers. When a chorus effect is added to a single singer, it sounds a bit like many people are singing (as in a classical chorus).

- *Flange:* A continually sweeping, variable, short delay (under 20 milliseconds) that causes moving comb filtering functions.

Figure 8.29: Kind of Loud/Universal Audio's Realverb, a reverb plug-in.

Figure 8.30: T.C. Electronic M3000 hardware reverb.

- *Pitch:* Pitch processors adjust the frequency of incoming signals. They can be used to create harmonies, basic chorusing, and suboctaves. Processors that also sense the frequency of the incoming signal can be programmed to automatically correct notes that are out of tune. While most popular on vocals, these effects can create very cool sounds when used on instruments. Suboctaves sound great on kick drum and bass, but even vocals and guitar can occasionally benefit. Snare drum timbres can also be filled out with some careful pitch manipulations.

Many other effects can be useful in the studio. Distortions of various kinds are sometimes used on vocals, guitars, and kick and snare drums. Emulator effects attempt to copy, through virtual means, the sonic characteristics of hardware devices such as guitar amps, microphones, classic compressors, reverbs, synthesizers, and tape machines.

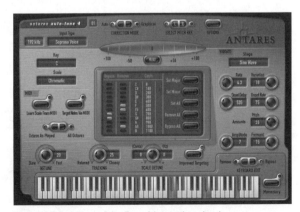

Figure 8.31: Antares Auto-Tune 4 intonation plug-in.

Figure 8.32: Kind of Loud/Universal Audio's Nigel, a guitar amp simulator plug-in.

Dynamics

Dynamics processors automatically adjust signal level based on a series of user-defined parameters. Dynamics are not always classified as effects since the outcome can vary from subtle level adjustments (performing a sort of automated mixing) to a complete reshaping of a sound. Because of their great flexibility and wide array of possible uses, dynamics processors are an essential part of any studio. Many professional studios have more than two per recording channel, which is a lot cheaper to accomplish in the software domain as compared to buying dedicated hardware units. Some basic types of dynamics processing are listed below.

- *Compression:* Lowers the level of an incoming signal when it exceeds a preset point (called the threshold). The end result is a decrease in dynamic range. Compression is used to even out the dynamic contour of a performance. It can increase the average output level of an individual track or of the entire mix. Extreme settings can even adjust the timbre of the sound itself.

- *Limiting:* An extreme form of compression where the signal level is drastically reduced (in a ratio of greater than 10:1) when the input exceeds a preset point. Peak limiting, even more extreme, does not exceed a preset level regardless of the level of the input signal. It is most often used to prevent clipping and in final mastering.

- *Gating:* Only allows signal that exceeds a preset level (threshold) to pass. Anything lower than the threshold is not passed to the output and is replaced by silence. Gates are often used to remove noise from a track when the performer is not playing. Gating the output of a reverb is also a popular effect, as it can be used to create a very large sound that disappears quickly.

Figure 8.33: TL Audio Fat 1 hardware compressor.

- *Expansion:* Lowers the noise floor and increases dynamic range by either reducing the signal that is below a preset threshold, or increasing the signal that rises above the threshold. Expansion can be a less obvious way to reduce noise than using a gate.

- *Ducking:* Utilizes a second input (side chain) to trigger the compression of a signal entering the primary input (program). This is most often used to reduce the level of a bass line (program) when the kick drum hits (side chain), the level of electric guitars (program) when the vocals are present (side chain), and the level of a music bed and sound effects (program) when narration or dialogue (side chain) needs to stand out.

Figure 8.34: Focusrite ISA 130+110 software compressor plug-in.

Figure 8.35: Digidesign Smack software compressor plug-in.

- *De-essing:* A frequency-dependent form of ducking used to reduce momentary frequency-specific peaks in the audio signal. This is accomplished by sending the same audio to both program and side-chain inputs. The signal entering the side chain, however, is subjected to a drastic form of EQ to increase the frequencies that need to be lowered in the program signal. When these selected frequencies exceed the threshold, the program material is quickly lowered. De-essers are most often used for removing pops, clicks, and sibilance (hard consonant sounds in vocal tracks).

Mastering Gear

Mastering is the final step in preparing a sound recording for duplication, release, and distribution. It is the art of creating a definitive version that will sound its best on (and is most suitable for) the intended delivery format and playback environment. This is accomplished by using EQ, pitch, dynamic, phase, and format manipulations. Mastering can be done at home, but it is often better to leave this last stage to a professional mastering engineer who has the proper equipment and experience to know what's best. In addition, they can lend an objective, fresh ear to the project during its crucial final stages. The acoustics and equipment used in a mastering house must be of the highest quality and are very expensive. Recordings released on major labels or large independents are almost always mastered at dedicated mastering facilities by engineers specializing in this area. The vast majority of current lower-budget recordings, however, are mastered in the same studio in which they are mixed.

While individual mastering components can be purchased separately and assembled in both hardware and software, there are numerous integrated solutions for the budget-conscious project studio. They incorporate high-quality limiting, compression, dither, format conversion, noise reduction, EQ, and imaging control. Popular hardware units are available from Focusrite, Drawmer, dbx, and T.C. Electronic. Software vendors include IK Multimedia, Waves, Arboretum Systems, Isotope, Steinberg, T.C. Electronic, and Digidesign. Digital mastering gear should be at least 24-bit capable (at 96kHz or a greater sample rate if needed).

Cabling & Connectors

One of the most commonly overlooked parts of a clean signal chain (and, therefore, recording) is the cabling and connectors. This is a place where people are tempted to cut corners and use the least expensive options. I'll say this once: Use the good stuff! Don't sacrifice sound quality just to save $12 on a cable. You'll regret it later. Good cable costs more due to the amount and quality of metals, jacketing, and other components used. You don't have to buy the most expensive cables—just not the bargain stuff.

With the exception of speaker wire and instrument cables, use equipment, cabling, and connectors that are shielded and have three conductors per audio channel (called a balanced connection) whenever possible. These maintain audio quality much better and can be run farther than unbalanced (two-pin) connections. Acceptable common connectors include XLR and ¼-inch TRS (tip-ring-sleeve). Avoid ¼-inch TS, RCA, or ⅛-inch mini connectors as these are unbalanced connectors only.

Be aware that connectors with three contacts can be used as either balanced or unbalanced depending on how they are wired and to which equipment they are attached. A three-conductor cable attached to the unbalanced output of a CD player will not balance the signal. If the signal is unbalanced anywhere in the path, the entire path is unbalanced, regardless of the cabling used. A special circuit (as found in DIs or line amplifiers) must be used to balance the output of an unbalanced device if the audio is to travel more than five feet. Often, line drivers will also convert the signal from −10dBV to +4dBm operation.

Avoid using adapters. These add noise to the signal and often can skew the frequency response as well. There is also a risk of unbalancing the signal or even inverting its phase. Use cabling manufactured with the correct connections and cable type required for your system.

That being said, every studio should be loaded with adapters and spare cables with assorted end connectors. These are for emergencies only (of which there will be plenty) and should not be permanently installed in any part of the studio. They are essential, however, when clients need to interface some special equipment they brought or some of your normal cabling goes bad. Unexpected downtime or the inability to connect various audio devices can quickly be the death of any studio.

Below are a number of the most common audio connectors and their possible uses.

Figure 8.36: Neutrik NF2C-B-2 RCA connectors.

- *RCA:* Two-conductor connectors usually used for −10dBV "consumer" unbalanced line-level audio signals. They are also used to make S/PDIF digital audio (or sometimes word clock) connections, but through different cable, more similar to video cabling (these may look the same as analog audio cabling, but they are not—do not substitute).

Figure 8.37: Neutrik NBNC75 BNC connector.

- *BNC:* Two-conductor connectors most commonly used to make S/PDIF digital audio, word clock, or video connections.

Figure 8.38: Neutrik NP2X ¼-inch TS connector.

- *¼-inch TS* (tip/sleeve, a.k.a. phone): Two-conductor connectors used to connect unbalanced line-level audio (usually at the −10 dBV consumer standard), high-impedance instrument, or even high-power speaker signals. Again, since these various purposes actually require different wire cable, instrument (hi-Z), speaker, and line-level audio cables are not interchangeable.

Figure 8.39: Neutrik NP3X ¼-inch TRS connector.

- *¼-inch TRS* (tip/ring/sleeve): Three-conductor connectors commonly used to connect balanced line-level audio signals (usually at the +4dBm "professional" standard). Beware that these can also be used in an unbalanced mono fashion or as insert cables (a.k.a. Y or send/return cables). In this configuration, the opposite end splits off into two cables that terminate in ¼-inch TS connectors. These cables are capable of sending two unbalanced audio signals, either as stereo or dual mono. When used specifically as insert cables, one side is used for in, the other for out. You can also use ¼-inch TRS connectors for unbalanced stereo headphone connections, requiring yet another type of wire cable.

- *XLR* (cannon): Most commonly found on mic cables as well as +4dBm professional line-level audio cables. XLRs are also used for digital audio connections using the AES/EBU standard. Note that the cabling used for AES/EBU is not the same as either mic or line-level cables.

Figure 8.40: Neutrik NC3MXX_Ni XLR (male) connector.

Figure 8.41: Neutrik NC3FXX_Ni XLR (female) connector.

- *Combo:* Three-conductor input jacks that can accept either XLR or ¼-inch connectors. In order to offer greater I/O possibilities on smaller and smaller audio interfaces, manufacturers are increasingly relying on these jacks.

Figure 8.42: Neutrik NP3TT-1-B bantam (TT) connectors.

- *TT* (tiny telephone or bantam): Three-conductor connectors used to connect balanced line-level audio signals (usually at the +4dBm professional standard). These are of a smaller diameter than ¼-inch jacks and so are used to save space.

- *Mini TS:* Two-conductor connectors usually used for –10dBV consumer unbalanced line-level audio signals. These are most common on older computers and synthesizers.

- *Mini TRS:* Three-conductor connectors usually used for stereo –10dBV consumer unbalanced line-level audio signals. With two mini TS connectors on the other end of the cable, mini TRS connectors are common for stereo connections on computers and portable CD, DVD, MP3, and MD players. These connectors can also be used to make balanced mono connections.

Figure 8.43: Neutrik NTP3RC 3.5-mm tiny connector (male).

Figure 8.44: Neutrik NLT4FX Speakon connector.

- *Banana:* Two-conductor connectors used for high-power speaker cable.

- *Speakon:* Two-conductor connectors used for high-power speaker cable. These connectors twist and lock in place, and so are used widely for live sound reinforcement.

- *Raw* (no connectors): Two-conductor speaker wire is sometimes just left raw on the ends (without connectors) when the speakers and/or amp have binding posts, clamps, or tabs to connect to.

- *D-sub:* A widely used multipin connector, most often with 25 or 50 pins. Normally used for multichannel balanced audio.

- *Elco:* A multipin connector made famous by the ADAT standard, in which it was a 56-pin format. Normally used for multichannel balanced audio.

- *Optical:* Another common method for the transmission of digital audio is through optical lines. These are most often two-channel S/PDIF-type signals or eight-channel Lightpipe variations, though studios are beginning to rely on optical data lines to connect everything.

A Note on Phase

In most places, including the U.S., the standard for wiring audio connections and cables is that pin two is hot (positive), pin three is cold (negative), and pin one is ground on XLR cabling. Balanced TRS lines are supposed to be: tip = hot, ring = cold, and sleeve = ground. Be sure to check all equipment and cabling to determine if it matches these conventions. You may still find different wiring configurations on equipment from abroad or on older gear. Sometimes manufacturers just make good, old-fashioned mistakes, as hundreds of tiny wires and connectors tend to look alike after a while to those assembling mass quantities. In fact, a cable tester is a must have for any studio. There are a few on the market these days that check continuity, wiring schemes, and even intermittency (loose connections).

Mixdown Media, Backup & Storage

When a multitrack recording is ready for a final mix, it must be made into a final stereo or multichannel surround version that is often sent to a mastering facility or directly to a pressing plant. This used to mean recording the mix to either ¼-inch or ½-inch analog tape until both DAT and PCM-1630 digital tape methods became more popular. Now it is not uncommon to use an audio CD-R or, even better, a PMCD (premaster CD). In fact, to simplify final mastering, the audio data files can be stored on CD-ROMs, DVD-Rs, or removable hard drives. CD-Rs or DVD-Rs are also good media for backing up sessions. Many bands who self-publish their music prefer these formats.

After a project is over, create one or more backups. Include all original media files, session files, MIDI files, and documentation. It's not a bad idea to also create an OMF (open media file) version of the session, which is a bit more compatible across platforms and software programs. Similarly, all software-specific MIDI files should also be saved as general MIDI files. The idea here is that you or someone else could open this session in the future and get it all going again quickly.

All backup media should be archived in a safe location and contain the following information on both the case and directly on the media itself:

- Artist(s).

- Label and producer.

- Engineer(s).

- Date(s).

- Song titles and durations.

- Recording/mixing platform(s).

- Bit depth/sample rate.

Instruments

Having a small selection of high-quality instruments (real and virtual) and amplifiers available, while not a necessity, can aid tremendously in the quality of recordings produced at the studio. In addition, the visual and functional allure of this gear can help sell studio time.

Auxiliary percussion instruments such as guiro, vibraslap, tambourine, claves, flexitone, shakers, dumbek, congas, djembe, cowbells, and brake drums can add interest and flavor to a mix and are relatively inexpensive.

Of course owning a decent, well-tuned drum kit can also be useful. Some bands just starting out have absolutely atrocious instruments. Even just a professional-level studio snare, kick, and hi-hat can help.

While half and full speaker stacks for guitar are visually stunning, a flexible but small combo amplifier is often all that is needed to get great tone in the studio when it is properly recorded with the right microphone and preamp.

Electronic keyboards are a great addition, as is a real grand piano, if you can afford it. A few MIDI synthesizers and samplers can come in very handy and attract clients. Beware, however: Studio engineers should familiarize themselves with these and be prepared to use them if called upon.

Drum machines are invaluable when dealing with a drummer with a crummy kit. The sounds of the real kit can be enhanced (or even replaced!) by much nicer electronic versions. Electronic drums also make it easy to edit the performance itself!

DIs & Instrument Interfaces

A DI (direct inject) is a device designed to interface electronic instruments and amplifiers with either the mic or line inputs found on consoles or microphone preamplifiers. Professional studios should be equipped with a number of DIs.

The most useful ones offer three basic functions for doing this:

- Selectable reduction of the signal level.

- Balancing high-impedance, unbalanced sources and reducing the impedance to the range required by most consoles.

- Isolating the input signal from the output in order to reduce the likelihood of the audible hum associated with ground loops.

Figure 8.45: Behringer DI 100 direct inject (DI) box.

Recently a surge of specialty DIs has hit the market. These offer limited computer interfaces, amp modeling, guitar modeling, vocal effects, microphone modeling, impedance switching, reamp interfacing, and more. If buying one of these, just be sure it offers the audio quality and regular DI features you need.

MIDI Interfaces, Synthesizers, Samplers & Sequencers

MIDI (Musical Instrument Digital Interface) is a communications protocol used to connect musical devices such as keyboards, synthesizers, drum machines, and samplers. It can also be used to synchronize equipment or control technical parameters of their function. MIDI messages can be recorded and played back by a sequencer. Most current professional DAWs have sequencing functions built in. These can be used to control and record performances of the studio's MIDI instruments. They are a must-have.

MIDI allows a computer to communicate with any outboard MIDI device. For a software sequencer to communicate with a MIDI keyboard, for instance, an interface must make the translation. MIDI interfaces come with various options including SMPTE striping and sync. All studios should have interfaces with plenty of inputs and outputs. Each should be separately addressable from within the software, offering 16 separate MIDI channels on each connection.

Control Surfaces

As computer-based recording and mixing has become more powerful and widespread in the professional community, the general inadequacy of the mouse as an input device has become increasingly evident. When mixing 24 or more tracks with panning, effects, and dynamics, a single-reference input device does not offer the flexibility or tactile feedback that traditional consoles and outboard gear do. To combat this, some manufacturers are now offering physical control surfaces. These devices look like mixing consoles and have multiple faders, knobs, and buttons to control the virtual mixer.

A secondary benefit of using these devices is the "wow" factor. Studios that have forgone the dedicated mixer for a computer-based interface do not make as great a visual impression upon clients. Control surfaces with moving faders bring back some of this visual stimulation.

Control surfaces basically fit into two categories: control only and control/mixer. Control-only devices do not actually route audio signals directly. Without being connected to a computer or other host, they can accomplish no mixing or processing of audio. Control/mixers, on the other hand, combine external control of a host's functions with their own audio processing. They may offer mixing, effects, microphone preamplifiers, conversion, interfacing, EQ, dynamics, MIDI, synchronization, and more.

Current control surfaces are offered by Tascam, Digidesign/Focusrite, Mackie, Roland, and JL Cooper.

Clocking & Sync

When digital audio information moves in real time from one machine to another, it is often sent using one of the following transfer protocols: AES/EBU, S/PDIF, Lightpipe, TDIF, R-BUS, or MADI. An extremely large amount of data must be sent very rapidly in order to accomplish this in real time: Millions to trillions of bits are sent per minute from one machine to the next serially, and they all must send and receive each bit at the same time and rate. If the rates vary and one machine goes slower than the other, the information becomes out of sync. What one machine sends as the first bit of an audio word may be interpreted as the last bit of the previous one by a second, receiving machine. This can cause one machine (or both) to stop, play horrible noise, or generate loud, intermittent click sounds.

To ensure this does not happen, all of the aforementioned digital audio protocols have a built-in clocking signal (referred to as digital sync). One machine, the master, uses its internal clock to time the sending of its samples. The second machine is then set to listen to the timing signal (digital clock) from that first machine and advance its clock in unison. This works fine for the simplest setups, but problems quickly arise when more machines are added—in addition to the problems listed above, the sound can be played at the wrong speed/pitch.

When a studio has three or more audio devices connected digitally (through one of the protocols mentioned above), a common clock reference becomes difficult to maintain. Each machine has both digital inputs and outputs and they are all interconnected, like a spider web; with everything linked it is hard to determine which digital sync signal is from the master machine and which is from the slaves. The task is even more difficult if various delays are introduced. In order to solve this problem, most studios utilize a separate clocking signal, called word clock, that is not a part of the audio chain. It does not carry any information other than a timing clock to be used as a sync signal. A dedicated word-clock generator can be connected to all of the gear both separately and directly, and is an essential part of any studio sending digital audio signals around to and from various pieces of gear.

Figure 8.46: Apogee Big Ben digital clock generator.

SMPTE (Society of Motion Picture and Television Engineers) and MTC (MIDI time code) are two other methods of synchronization. While not as accurate as digital sync or word clock, both SMPTE and MTC contain information about the exact location in time, expressed in frames. Digital sync and word clock communicate a rate but not a location in time. SMPTE can be communicated and recorded as an audio signal (called LTC, or longitudinal time code) or as a time stamp on videotape (called VITC, or vertical interval time code).

Other, more proprietary types of synchronization are specific to certain makes and models of equipment. ADAT sync and Sony nine-pin sync are two of the most popular. Neither carries audio, but both do carry machine control functions, time location, and sync information.

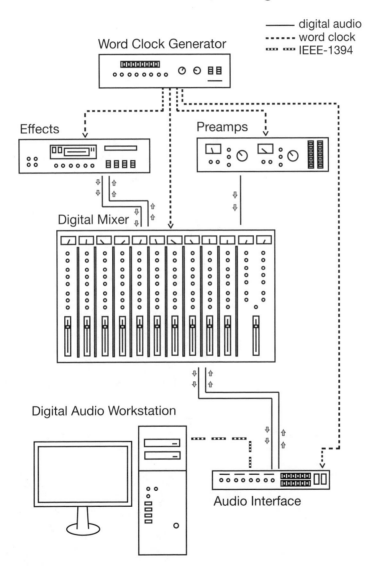

Figure 8.47: Digital clocking diagram.

Chapter Summary

1. Before designing a studio or purchasing recording equipment, you need to fully understand the necessary elements. With all of the options and technologies now available, integration of components can be both difficult and confusing…in some instances even impossible. Compatibility issues are therefore paramount.

2. When designing a studio and choosing specific types of gear, be sure to consider what types of jobs and clientele the studio will handle. This is especially true with regard to MIDI instruments and implementation, video synchronization capabilities, microphone quantity and types, audio interfaces, and mastering equipment.

3. In modern digital recording studios, audio quality can be quite high. Unfortunately, studio owners often overlook a number of important issues specific to this new technology and therefore compromise the studio's fidelity. It is critical that you understand and properly address latency, clocking, and synchronization.

4. Even in digital recording studios, analog audio elements are unavoidable. They are present in microphones, preamps, electronic instruments, cabling, and converters. All analog elements should be well integrated and of high enough quality to maintain a professional level of fidelity.

5. Create diagrams, charts, and outlines of the full signal flow of the studio before purchasing studio equipment. Include analog audio, digital audio, MIDI, and all clocking and synchronization signals.

9. Example Studio Setups

After reading this chapter, you should be able to:
- Understand what equipment is needed to complete a studio within a certain budget range.
- Create an outline specific to your individual needs.

This chapter offers examples of studio setups within specific price ranges. The studios listed would cost around $26,000, $75,000, and $150,000 to set up from scratch. Within a given price range there are countless options in platform/hardware combinations, and exactly which you use is a matter of personal preference. The setups given below are merely intended to get the thought process going.

All of these studios are based around digital technology, as it offers the most power with the lowest price tag. In addition, since digital technology is the current state of the industry, it is necessary to be compatible with others in the field.

The studios below have a minimum of 16 simultaneous inputs (mic or line) and are fully 24-bit compatible. They all support over 100 tracks (CPU and operating system permitting).

The prices listed for specific equipment are mostly MAP prices, which are the minimum advertised prices. These figures are close to "street prices," but actual asking prices may vary slightly in either direction. When manufacturers do not supply MAP pricing, I have given suggested list. "Street" will be much less than list. All prices are current as of mid-2005. Also, keep in mind that all computers listed will become outmoded very fast. They can easily be swapped for the latest cool model, however, often at a similar price.

These outlines are thorough, but not exhaustive. As with any long, complex equipment list, there are bound to be oversights, however small (or large).

Under $30,000

This studio design gives 18 tracks of input at a time at 24 bits and up to 192kHz! It has a nice mic collection, a powerful computer, and great DAW software. The preamps and converters are top quality. This is absolutely amazing bang for the buck.

Basic Outline

Recording platform: Cubase

Inputs (simultaneous): 18

Outputs (simultaneous): 6

Number of tracks (maximum): 200

Monitoring: stereo

Mic preamps: 20

Effects: host-based

Analog to digital converters: 24 bit, 192kHz

Digital to analog converters: 24 bit, 192kHz

Mixer: software

The Setup

Gear	Quantity	Price
Workstation		
Compaq 800T 3.4 GHz Pentium 4, 320-GB Raid 0 hard drive, DVD-RW, CD, 1 GB RAM		$1,740
ViewSonic G810B monitor		$445
Lynx 2B audio card (with cables)		$899
Lynx AES16 audio card (with cables)		$699
Software		
Cubase 3.0		$599
Waves Native Gold Bundle		$975
Cycling 74 Pluggo		$169
Antares Auto-Tune, v. 4		$320
Studio Furniture		
Raxxess ERK-20M		$179
Workstation computer table		$300
Monitor pedestals		$200
Raxxess IsoRaxx GR30		$1,050

Gear	Quantity	Price
Mic Preamps and Converters		
Focusrite ISA 428 (with digital I/O card)		$2,300
Cabling for ISA 428		$65
RME OctaMic D		$1,179
SM Pro Audio PR8MK-II		$200
Tape Machines		
Sony TCW565R dual cassette deck		$270
Monitors		
Event 20/20BAS v.2	pair	$900
Headphones		
Beyerdynamic DT770 Pro	$150 each x 2	$300
AKG K240S	$99 each x 3	$297
AKG K55	$30 each x 3	$90
Oz Audio Qmix		$280
Hosa HPE325 extension cable	$8.50 each x 4	$34
Power		
Furman PM-Pro II power conditioner		$340
APC BackUp1400 UPS		$550
Power strips	$10 each x 5	$50
Extension cords (14 gauge, 12 ft.)	$8 each x 3	$24
Extension cords (14 gauge, 25 ft.)	$13 each x 2	$26
Microphones		
Shure drum mic kit: Beta 52, A56D (x 3), SM57 (x 3)		$459
Neumann KM184		$730
Crown CM700MP	matched pair	$499
Shure SM57	$80 each x 2	$160
AKG D112		$220
Shure SM58	$100 each x 2	$200
Neumann TLM103		$999
Audio-Technica 4040		$300
Audio-Technica 4041		$300
Audio-Technica DR-1000 (for talkback)		$29
Microphone Accessories		
Pro-Co 20-MIC-XX-SQ mic cable, 20 ft.	$34 each x 20	$680

Gear	Quantity	Price
Microphone Accessories		
K+M boom stand	$50 each x 12	$600
Atlas DMS10E stands	$23 each x 2	$46
Atlas PB11XE booms	$38 each x 2	$76
Quik-Lok A-341BK short tripod with tele-boom	$40 each x 4	$160
Stereo mic bar, adjustable		$18
Raxxess POMT8, 8-in. plosive filter	$23 each x 2	$46
Instruments		
Korg X5D keyboard/synth		$600
Line 6 PodXT		$299
Midiman Midisport 4x4 USB MIDI interface		$149
DIs		
Behringer DI 100	$35 each x 2	$70
Countryman DI		$155
Miscellaneous		
Neutrik NYS-SPP: 48-point, 1/4-in. TRS patch bay		$145
Mogami SS03: 1/4-in. TRS patch cables, 3-ft. x 8	$11.50 each x 8	$92
Hosa CSS845: 1/4-in. TRS patch cables, 1.5-ft., eight-pack		$23
Behringer CT 100 cable tester		$55
Main snakes with connectors and wall jacks		$600
		Subtotal $22,190
Acoustics		
Auralex MoPADs		$30
Auralex Roominators D108L		$599
Standard model isolation booth (4 ft. x 6 ft. x 7 ft., 2 in.) with extra window		$3,200
Gobos, homemade		$175
		Total $26,194

Under $80,000

This intermediate-level studio is built around an Apogee/Logic Pro system. It uses the host CPU for its processing. It has more DIs, MIDI, synthesis, all-round great converters, 24-bit/96kHz, a mix control surface, and loads of plug-ins. In addition, there's a larger budget for the studio space and acoustics.

Basic Outline

Recording platform: Logic Pro

Inputs (simultaneous): 16

Outputs (simultaneous): 16

Number of tracks (maximum): 192

Monitoring: stereo

Mic preamps: 18

Effects: host-based

ADC: 24 bit, 96kHz

DAC: 24 bit, 96kHz

Mixer: software with control surface

The Setup

Gear	Quantity	Price
Workstation		
Apple Macintosh G5 Dual 2.5 GHz		$2,999
Sony SDM-HS93/B 19-in. LCD display	$619 each x 2	$1,238
Apogee Rosetta 800 96K 8x8 channel interface	$2,695 each x 2	$5,390
Apogee X-Firewire 800 (Firewire option for Rosetta 800)	$539 each x 2	$1,078
Mackie Control Surface		$999
Mackie Control Extender		$849
Emagic Amt8 MIDI interface		$369
Software		
Apple Logic Pro		$999
Bias Peak 4		$399
Waves Platinum Bundle Native		$1,575
Antares Auto-Tune Native		$319
UAD1 Ultra Pak		$1,199

Gear	Quantity	Price
Software		
Waves IR1 Native Convolution Reverb		$600
Native Instruments Komplete2		$999
Studio Furniture		
Omnirax Force 36		$1,699
Outboard Gear		
PreSonus Digimax96	$1,329 each x 2	$2,658
PreSonus DM007 Digimax AES/EBU breakout cable		$24
Universal Audio 2-610		$1,899
FMR Audio RNC	$175 each x 2	$350
Behringer DI 100	$29 each x 2	$58
Line6 Pod XT		$299
Line6 Bass Pod XT		$299
Monitors		
Event Precision 8 Active	$649 each x 2	$1,298
Roland MA8		$89
PreSonus Central Station		$499
PreSonus CSR-1		$149
Headphones and Cue		
Sony MDR7506		$99
AKG K240S		$99
Behringer HPS5000	$34 each x 6	$204
Hear Technologies Hub		$375
Hear Technologies Mixer	$150 each x 4	$600
Instruments		
Yamaha Motif ES rack		$1,099
Korg Triton Studio 76		$2,999
Fender American Strat		$929
Gibson Les Paul Studio		$1,199
Fender American P-Bass		$999
Marshall DSL100		$1,499
Marshall 1960AV 4x12 with 30-watt vintage 30s		$949

Gear	Quantity	Price
Microphones		
Shure SM57	$89 each x 4	$356
Shure Beta52		$189
Shure SM58	$99 each x 2	$198
AKG C414 B XL II		$840
Shure SM81	$349 each x 2	$698
AKG D112		$199
Sennheiser MD421	$329 each x 2	$658
Rode NT1A		$199
Rode NT5		$399
Microphone Accessories		
Atlas LO-2 stand adapters	$12 each x 10	$120
K&M 21090B	$55 each x 4	$220
K&M 25900B	$55 each x 3	$165
Ultimate MC05	$19 each x 4	$76
Quik-Lok A50	$110 each x 2	$220
20-ft. mic cables	$20 each x 15	$300
25-ft. mic cables	$22 each x 15	$330
K&M 23510B hinged mic bar		$17
K&M 22400B 12-in. gooseneck	$23 each x 3	$69
Power		
Furman SB-1000 UPS		$599
Furman IT-1220		$1,210
Misc. power strips and extension cords		$80
Miscellaneous		
dbx PB25 patch bay	$129 each x 2	$258
Custom 16-channel snake		$595
TRS patch cables, 2 ft.	$12 each x 15	$180
Guitar stands	$25 each x 2	$50
Subtotal		**$47,608**
Construction and Acoustics		**$30,000**
Total		**$77,608**

Under $175,000

The higher studio level here is built around the flagship Pro Tools HD system. It can use either the host CPU or its own maxed-out DSP chips for processing. It has some amazing converters and mic pres, works at 24-bit/192kHz, and includes tons of fantastic plug-ins. Of all the studios so far, this one also has the most visual pizzazz. This studio, however, also requires the largest budget yet for acoustics and the procurement of a good studio facility.

Basic Outline

Recording platform: Pro Tools HD 3

Inputs (simultaneous): 24

Outputs (simultaneous): 24

Number of tracks (max): 192

Monitoring: stereo

Mic preamps: 21

Effects: host-based and DSP

ADC: 24 bit, 192kHz

DAC: 24 bit, 192kHz

Mixer: software, control surface/analog mixer

The Setup

Gear	Quantity	Price
Workstation		
Apple Macintosh G5 Dual 2.5 GHz		$2,999
Apple 23-in. Cinema display		$1,999
Digidesign 192 I/O Pro Tools HD 16-channel interface	$3,995 each x 2	$7,990
Digidesign 192 A/D 8-channel analog expansion		$1,295
Digidesign Control 24 Pro Tools control surface (16 preamps)		$7,995
Emagic Amt8 MIDI interface		$369
Software		
Digidesign Pro Tools HD3		$12,995
Apple Logic Pro		$999
Bias Peak 4		$399
Waves Platinum TDM Bundle		$4,200
Antares Auto-Tune Native		$319

Gear	Quantity	Price
Software		
AudioEase Altiverb TDM		$699
Native Instruments Komplete2		$999
Propellerheads Reason		$449
Fxpansion BFD		$299
Fxpansion BFD XFL		$249
Studio Furniture		
Argosy 90-C24-RR control 24 console		$2,060
Quik-Lok Z726L		$199
Outboard Gear		
Avalon VT737		$1,995
Avalon U5	$540 each x 2	$1,080
Universal Audio 2-610		$1,899
Grace Design 201		$1,850
Behringer DI100	$29 each x 2	$58
T.C. Electronic M3000		$1,499
Universal Audio 2-1176	$2,395 each x 2	$4,790
FMR Audio RNC	$175 each x 2	$350
Monitors		
Genelec 8050A	$1,749 each x 2	$3,498
Event TR5	$150 each x 2	$300
Headphones and Cue		
Sony MDR7506	$99 each x 3	$297
AKG K240S	$99 each x 3	$297
Fostex T20	$70 each x 3	$210
Hear Technologies Hub		$375
Hear Technologies Mixer	$150 each x 4	$600
Instruments		
Korg Triton Studio 88		$3,399
Yamaha Motif ES 7		$2,499
Roland FantomXR		$1,345
Microphones		
Shure SM57	$89 each x 4	$356
Shure Beta52		$189

Gear	Quantity	Price
Microphones		
Shure SM58	$99 each x 2	$198
Shure Beta98/DS	$229 each x 3	$687
Shure SM81	$349 each x 2	$698
AKG D112		$199
Sennheiser MD421	$329 each x 2	$658
Neumann SKM184		$1,449
Neumann U87 Set/Z		$2,749
Rode K2		$699
Rode NT1A	$199 each x 2	$398
Microphone Accessories		
Atlas LO-2 stand adapters	$12 each x 20	$240
K&M 21090B	$55 each x 4	$220
K&M 25900B	$55 each x 3	$165
Ultimate MC05	$19 each x 4	$76
Quik-Lok A50	$110 each x 2	$220
20-ft. mic cables	$20 each x 15	$300
25-ft. mic cables	$22 each x 15	$330
K&M 23510B hinged mic bar		$17
K&M 22400B 12-in. gooseneck	$23 each x 3	$69
Power		
Furman SB-1000 UPS		$599
Furman IT-1220		$1,210
Misc. power strips and extension cords		$80
Miscellaneous		
dbx PB25 patch bay	$129 each x 2	$258
Custom 16-channel snake		$595
TRS patch cables, 2 ft.	$12 each x 15	$180
Guitar stands	$25 each x 2	$50
D-sub snakes	$90 each x 5	$450
Eight-channel TRS to TRS	$90 each x 8	$720
Subtotal		**$92,213**
26x30-ft. preplan building (www.menards.com)		$5,300
Other construction and acoustics		$75,000
Total		**$172,513**

Part I I

Running Your Studio

10. Marketing

After reading this chapter, you should be able to:
- Determine what your customers' needs are and how to create a competitive edge through niche marketing.
- Develop an effective marketing mix.
- Understand the various stages of a studio and the best way to use marketing in each stage.

Marketing is an essential part of any business operation. Its only goal is to attract customers to your recording studio who are willing to pay for your services. This chapter will take you through the basic steps of marketing, from market analysis to advertising campaigns.

Marketing is a powerful way to influence people's purchasing decisions. An effective marketing plan allows you to reach a targeted audience for the lowest possible price. The first step in creating your marketing plan is to understand your customers.

Today's customers are extremely demanding and have access to vast amounts of information. They are, for the most part, price and quality sensitive. Therefore, recording studios must deliver quality products at a price that satisfies customers, while keeping costs down to make a profit. Not an easy task!

Many factors influence our buying behavior, including the culture and social class to which we belong, and the views of our reference group—family, friends, and peers. Self

Facts About the U.S. Market

- The United States absorbs (in dollar terms) about 30 percent of all the recorded music produced.

- Demand for recorded music fluctuates cyclically and is sensitive to economic trends.

- A strong market for recorded music is related to an expanding teenage/young adult population and a thriving middle class.

- The recording industry relies on national advertising media with steady prices and performance improvements in audio hardware and recording technologies.

- Changes in the system of distributing music have an important effect on the industry's sales.

image is an important factor too. Consumers (particularly teenagers and younger people) purchase goods to express their identities. Marketing companies rely on endorsements from famous people for this reason.

When consumers buy a product, they go though five stages of decision making. A studio owner should design appropriate messages to help consumers reach the final stage.

1. Need recognition. At this stage, consumers recognize that they need a good or service. For example, a band may have written several songs and would like to have them professionally recorded.

2. Information search. At the second stage, consumers look for possible places to fulfill their need. Advertising via newspapers, magazines, the yellow pages, and the Internet are valid methods of attracting customers at this stage and providing information that is relevant to them.

3. Evaluation. After potential customers find information, they evaluate their options and look for the best quality, features, and price.

4. Purchase. Now the customer is ready to make a purchase. Here you need to reinforce the idea that the customer chose the correct studio.

5. Purchase outcome. This post-consumption stage is extremely important in maintaining customer loyalty and repeat purchases. You can follow up with customers through phone calls, warranties, newsletters, etc. What you need to avoid is buyer's remorse or cognitive dissonance, which occurs when a customer thinks about the other products they could have bought and concludes that they made a bad choice.

When you enter an established market, you need to set your studio apart from your competition. The first step is creating a brand identity, which comes from not only the studio name but a brand mark (a logo, symbol, or even the design of your packaging). A successful brand image helps customers recognize your studio in the long term. If customers develop an awareness of your brand, you may be able to charge higher prices for your service.

Companies often create a separate identity for each product that they sell. For example, the airline industry identifies each level of ticket with its own brand. If you travel in first class, you are in the "premier service," "upper class," or something along those lines. You can create a comparable system with your recording studio. If your studio offers different services based on price, you could create a premium name or identity that separates that service from your baseline service. Customers then recognize the benefits they receive from a particular service, without being confused by the options.

As you create your brand identities, register brand names and symbols with the Patent and Trademark Office. More information on how to register your brand is available in Chapter 12.

An effective marketing campaign is based on the well-balanced use of four components, often referred as the four P's: product, price, promotion, and place.

Product

A recording studio's product line includes not only tangible goods such as CDs but the services, ideas, and people in the studio. Therefore, your product line should include elements such as the services you provide, the features of your studio, benefits obtained by using your studio, and any guarantees or warranties that come with the final product. Your product line may also include other intangible elements such as the style and image created by your studio and any associated brand images. Extra benefits are important, too, such as free copies of masters, use of studio musical instruments, or free subscriptions to a recording studio newsletter. Combined, these elements will make a powerful impression on your current and potential customers.

Another factor in marketing your product is product positioning: distinguishing your product in the minds of your consumers. Product positioning emphasizes the strengths your studio has over its nearest rivals—for example, the highest quality in recording, the fastest service, any specialized services you offer, or the best advice and assistance available. To position your product, follow these steps:

1. Identify and analyze your competition, including the services that they provide and how they deliver these services.

2. Determine how consumers evaluate their options. Do they carefully consider the price, or are they primarily looking for a studio that has a proven record of accomplishment?

3. Look at how consumers perceive the competition. Do they see one company as a leader in your area? Do they dislike the services offered by your competition, or feel that their product is substandard?

4. Identify gaps in the competition's current position. Are they only interested in one style of music? Do they only want a certain type of client?

5. Analyze your unique abilities and qualities. What sets you and your products apart from the competition? Can you position this advantage in the eyes of your consumers and keep it there?

Price

Customers often rate a product or service on the price they must pay. Like any business owner, you must establish a pricing system that provides enough profit while attracting customers. Most studios establish a floor price as the basis of their pricing strategy, and they do not let the price go below this level because it would be lower than the cost of producing the product. Sometimes a studio does go below cost to attract customers and establish itself in a particular market, using strategies such as loss leading and penetration pricing (more on those below). No matter what you charge, though, your service must justify your prices.

An important question with regard to your pricing system is whether you will only charge cash for your services. If you offer credit card payment, consider what the cost to your studio will be. Will you need to add a surcharge to absorb the extra cost?

In determining the price of your products, you need to do the following:

- Define your costs, including material, labor (cost applied to make your product, including taxes), and overhead (indirect costs such as insurance, depreciation, rent, accounting, utilities, and advertising).

- Calculate the markup and margin. This is expressed as a percentage of the selling price. For example, if it costs $120 to record a song and you sell it to your customer for $160, the markup/margin is $40. The margin is 25 percent ($40 divided by $160), and the markup is 33⅓ percent ($40 divided by $120).

There are three standard pricing strategies:

- *Cost-plus pricing:* After assessing the cost of producing a good or service, you set a price that takes into account a markup percentage. As noted above, this markup must include direct and indirect costs.

- *Competitive pricing:* Your competition's pricing policy forms the basis of this strategy. Your goal is to set a price that is below their minimum price to attract a similar audience. This strategy is good for establishing your recording studio, but may lead to price wars between you and your nearest competitor. Furthermore, this strategy may not be profitable in the long term, as you may be reducing your profit margins too low.

- *Value-in-use pricing:* A complex strategy, value-in-use pricing relies on predicting the value of your service if it wasn't available. For example, what would it cost to produce an album if your customers had to drive 50 miles to the nearest studio?

Once you've adopted one of these pricing strategies, you need to choose a specific pricing method. Pricing methods are ways to fine-tune the amount you will charge for your products and services, and to attract customers by adding value to the services provided. Pricing methods traditionally fall into two categories based either on cost or benefits.

Cost-Based Methods

- *Skimming pricing:* This technique relies on setting initial prices high to recover capital spent on development or opening a new store. If you intend to use this method you need to focus attention on quality, service, or the uniqueness or your product, rather than the price. One problem with this method is that the competition may lower prices to beat you in the market.

- *Loss leader pricing:* With this method, you select one item and sell it below cost to create store traffic so you can sell other items at a regular price. For example, you may charge less for the recording time than your competitor, but you may have a greater markup in blank CDs to make up that difference. It is important that you have these loss-leader items on hand and are not trying to switch a customer to higher priced items.

- *Price point pricing:* Here, you price your products just below important thresholds for the buyer to give a perception of lower price. For example, $9.95 seems considerably lower than $10.05. This type of pricing is similar to odd pricing, in which you use pricing figures that end in five, seven, and nine. Consumers tend to round down the price of goods; for example, they round $29.95 down to $29 rather than up to $30, so they see the product in the $20 rather than $30 price range.

- *Free add-on pricing:* Here, you add free or nominal-cost items or services to your product to substantially increase the perceived value. Examples include delivery, updates, newsletters, e-mail notices, etc.

Benefits-Based Pricing

These benefits-based pricing methods emphasize the benefits of buying a product rather than the cost of producing it.

- *Cumulative quantity discount pricing:* With this method, you offer discounts based on the customers' accumulated purchases. For example, you give a discount to a customer if they use your studio for recording and mixing and for manufacturing the CD. This encourages loyalty and continued purchases.

- *Noncumulative quantity discount pricing:* This discount encourages purchasing more than one item per visit: for example, "Buy three, get the fourth free."

- *Promotional pricing:* With this method, you offer low prices for specific goods or services. Often new products are linked with other items, such as two-for-one specials or end-of-session specials. Promotional pricing stimulates demand and is useful in eliminating overstock.

- *Prestige and image pricing:* Here you offer the best product, free delivery, and added value to the product. Advertising should not mention price.

- *Pay one price:* You provide unlimited use of a service or product for one set price.

- *Differential pricing:* Your pricing is based on a particular segment of your market. For example, you may charge college students less for recording time in the hopes of generating greater numbers. Be careful not to violate any federal or state price discrimination laws when using this method.

- *Cash discount pricing:* With this method, you give discounts to customers who pay with cash rather than a check or credit card. This saves you billing and clerical costs including the premium charged by the bank.

Promotion

Promotion is the communication of information about your studio to customers to develop a favorable image in their minds. You achieve these goals by using a variety of promotional tools, including advertising, personal selling, sales promotion, and publicity and public relations.

Advertising

Advertising is paid, nonpersonal communication to a targeted market. The form of advertising varies according to the type of message you want to send to your customers. For example, when you are starting a studio, you need to rely on informative advertising, which creates awareness about your studio to potential customers and establishes a demand for your services. As your studio grows, your advertising message changes too. Other advertising techniques used by companies include:

- *Persuasive advertising:* This seeks to draw customers away from your rivals. It usually stresses aspects such as quality and price.

- *Comparative advertising:* This form of advertising directly compares your studio to another. Here you highlight any comparative advantages that your studio has over your nearest rival. You might emphasize price, equipment, clients, staff, and especially any awards and celebrities that have used your services.

- *Reminder advertising:* This advertising keeps your studio in the mind of your customers. Companies use this technique for repeat customers who have a favorable view of your services.

Personal Selling

Many recording studio owners overlook this important form of promotion. Personal selling is persuading customers to purchase goods through direct contact. Traditionally this method follows several stages:

- *Prospecting:* You identify potential customers through personal connections, friends, relatives, or business connections.

- *Approaching:* This stage occurs a few minutes after your first contact with the potential customer. Since this is a customer's first impression of your studio, it requires you to behave in a professional and courteous manner. This will help develop a positive image of your recording studio in a customer's mind.

- *Presenting and demonstrating:* Here you explain in detail the products and services that your studio can offer a customer. When talking to the customer you should concentrate on the benefits available if they use your studio.

- *Handling objections:* At this stage, you may have to deal with objections. These could take the form of inquiries on the benefits or services available or on pricing. Handling objections is very important for finalizing a sale.

- *Closing:* At this stage you ask the customer to purchase the product. You can either do this directly ("Why don't we book some time in the studio for next week?") or indirectly by implying that the sale is closed.

- *Follow-up:* Many companies feel that the relationship between the studio and the customer ends with the delivery of the final product, and they ignore this stage. However, successful studios spend the time to build lasting long-term relationships by calling customers to see if everything was to their liking. In addition, a studio should include these customers on mailing and newsletter lists, so the customer will remember the service.

Sales Promotion

Sales promotion involves short-term strategies that encourage customers to try new products or buy more of a certain product.

Coupons are an ideal incentive for customers. A coupon for free or discounted services can encourage a potential customer to try your studio. Coupons placed in print media, especially newspapers and magazines, often attract new customers. Another way to distribute coupons is to mail them to previous customers.

Premiums are free or reduced-price products that stimulate purchase. Examples include T-shirts, pens, mugs, and calendars given to customers in return for purchasing specific products.

Trade shows allow companies to display and demonstrate products to customers who have a special interest in a product or service. They are also ideal opportunities for companies to keep up with the latest developments in their field.

Publicity & Public Relations

Publicity and public relations both involve the communication of information to media outlets, but they are completely different in purpose and form.

Publicity is information presented in a news format, which customers often regard as objective and credible. However, studios have little control over the delivery and location of the message. Public relations seeks to build good relations with the community by performing and publicizing public-service activities. Both will be discussed in more detail in the next chapter.

Place

The last of the four P's, place, is the movement of goods from the studio to the customer. For most recording studios this is a very easy system. A studio produces the song or album and the customer comes and picks up their products.

You may also offer an ordering system for your customers. With this system, you transfer the recorded music to a CD manufacturer who then sends it directly to the customer. There are several things to consider in making such arrangements:

- Delivery time. How many days/weeks does it take a supplier to deliver merchandise to you or the customer? If there is a considerable time lag, customers may cancel their orders.

- Freight costs. Do you pay or does the supplier pay for freight?

- Reordering policy. Does the supplier require you to purchase a large amount, or can you purchase small numbers of items?

- Credit. What are the terms of the supplier's credit? What are the terms of buying?

For a studio there is the additional question of storage space. You may need to store goods received from a supplier before your customer picks them up. Do you have the space to receive such goods? Will your local zoning laws allow for delivery?

Chapter Summary

1. The goal of marketing is to attract customers to your recording studio. This is achieved by understanding the needs and wants of your customers, developing a marketing plan, and executing this plan via the correct media.

2. A successful marketing campaign relies on a well-balanced mix of product, price, place, and promotion.

3. Customers' expectations of a product are linked to its price. The price of a good or service is based on the cost of production and the profit margin that you want to create. You can use pricing strategies such as cost-plus pricing, competitive pricing, and value-in-use.

4. The goal of promotion is to build a positive image about a recording studio. This is achieved through paid communication such as advertising, and nonpaid communication such as personal selling, sales promotion, publicity, and public relations.

5. Place (distribution) is the movement of goods from a manufacturer to the consumer.

11. Advertising & Promotion

After reading this chapter, you should be able to:
- Understand and utilize the various types of advertising.
- Develop a successful advertising program with a controlled budget.
- Develop a targeted marketing campaign via appropriate media.
- Learn the tools of effective public relations.

Advertising is one of the most important elements of a successful recording studio. It creates awareness of the studio among potential clients and encourages demand for the studio's products and services. In addition, advertising helps to shape people's views of the music world, especially what they listen to and how they hear it. In advertising, though, you can't say or show anything that you wish. You must remain within the boundaries of the law (discussed later in chapter 12) and within the ethical and moral boundaries established by the government and trade associations.

Of all the promotional media available to you, advertising is the most effective method to reach a mass audience for the least amount of money. However, the studio still must operate within the boundaries of its budget and produce an advertising program that meets its needs.

Advertising Budgets

You should only consider advertising after establishing your studio's image, prices, and customer service. Furthermore, you should determine your goals as well as evaluate your recording studio's advantages over its nearest competitors by asking two simple questions:

1. What makes your studio different from or better than other studios in your region?

2. What facts about your studio should you tell potential customers?

Once you have answered these questions, you are ready to think about the form and cost of your advertising. Start with your local market and work outward to regional, state, and national markets. It is important to establish your local client base before looking for potential business in another area. Contact local media (newspapers, radio, TV, and direct mail printers) for information about services and results they offer.

An advertising worksheet (provided in the appendix) will help you figure your advertising costs over a period of 12 months. Check your results against other recording studios. Trade associations and other organizations often gather data on advertising expenses. If you see that your advertising expenses are greater than the average, you may have to take a second look at your advertising budget.

If the costs for advertising are still prohibitive, consider developing cooperative advertising, in which your studio and other businesses share the cost of an ad. This is usually done with local music merchants.

Advertising Messages

As mentioned previously, effective advertising requires you to know your target market and understand the objectives of the advertising campaign. Advertisements must be informative and truthful as well as credible and convincing.

In advertising, you need to catch the reader's attention by stressing the benefits of using your service. Start by creating a powerful headline. There are several types of headlines that are appropriate for your audience:

- News headline. For example: "New," "Announcing," or "Introducing"; "A new studio offers best recording in the region."

- How-to headline. This offers solutions, advice, and information. For example, "How to record a professional demo tape."

- Benefit headline. Offer a compelling reason for people to use your studio. For example, "Top quality mastering comes to XYZ without the high New York rates."

- Question headline. Focus on the customer's desires. For example, "Want to be a star? It all starts here."

- Testimonial headline. Use a customer's testimonial to sell your studio. For example, "Studio XYZ helped me get started in the music industry."

Remember that anyone reading your ad is wondering, "What is in it for me?" Get to the point fast, and appeal to people's self-interest through offers and incentives (for instance, the first session is free). Persuade them to take action right away. Place limits on your offers, and present a complete guarantee of satisfaction if they act now. Use language such as "Offer limited," "Act now," and "Get started today."

Advertising Media

You should advertise in the media that your target audience reads, listens to, or views. Furthermore, you should use media based on the return on investment of your advertisement.

For our purposes we will concentrate on eight media types: print, radio, fliers, classifieds, direct mail, television, point of sale, and yellow pages.

Print

Newspaper advertising is the most frequently used media for recording studios. Newspaper ads are often cheap and have short deadlines for submission that allow you to capitalize on any changes in your studio's marketing plan. Since most newspapers are daily, the exposure time of an ad is very short. To overcome this problem, studio owners typically use multiple insertions—regular exposure builds recognition and a better response. Another disadvantage of newspaper advertising is that most papers only cover a single community or metro area with a limited readership. Advertising in regional or national newspapers is often expensive and out of the reach of small studios.

Magazines have an advantage over newspapers in that they have specialized audiences. Each magazine concentrates its content and advertising on specific topics, and offers high production quality. Some popular examples include *Rolling Stone*, which deals with rock and popular music; *Guitar Player*, for musicians who play guitar; and *Jazz Times*, for jazz musicians. Magazines have an additional advantage in that many are monthly, thereby increasing the exposure time. This does mean that you must submit your ads well in advance, as lead times can be up to several months.

Trade publications are another important type of print media. Several newspapers and magazines deal with music industry issues and news. Examples include *Billboard* and, in the radio market, *Radio and Records* and *Gavin*. Trades can offer your studio a wonderful promotional outlet.

Several inexpensive options exist for print media advertising. You can place classified ads in local newspapers or magazines. Using local newspapers allows you to place small test ads before moving on to more expensive national media. For more on classified advertising, see below.

Radio

Radio is a key media outlet for the music industry. It is an excellent media for reaching teenagers and commuters within a definable market area. If you need to reach a broader market, it is important to understand how your recording studio matches the musical format of the station. Read the radio charts to find out which stations are more successful in your area.

A disadvantage of radio is the short length of the message. To remain in your target market's mind, you need to buy time consistently. To save money, you can run spot radio commercials in local markets. They are easy and inexpensive to record (often in your own studio) and broadcast.

Another alternative is noncommercial radio, including college radio, public radio, and community radio. Many stations accept donations for sponsorship or underwriting, so your costs are low and may be tax deductible. The disadvantage of college radio is the coverage. Most stations have a limited market, within a small region. Community radio, like college radio, operates with a community-based volunteer staff and a variety of programming suited to the local market. Since community radio is located in the AM bandwidth, the audience may be considerably smaller than what you would reach by other media.

Fliers

One of the cheapest and easiest forms of advertising is the flier. Fliers are ideal for placement on bulletin boards, under car windshield wipers, or in mailboxes. Apart from their low cost, fliers are an effective method for conveying information quickly to a potential audience. Flyer design must be simple, yet appealing. Use eye-catching colors. Keep your message brief, with tear sections that include your address, phone number, and e-mail address.

Classifieds

Classified ads offer a very economical way of reaching your audience. Furthermore, this form of advertising does not require demanding design or clever wording. Use as few words as possible, since you are paying for each word. Explain the benefits of using your studio, and use white space to make the ad visually appealing.

Many newspapers and magazines will assist you in constructing a classified ad. It is in your best interest to repeat the ad as often as possible. This will increase the chance that potential customers will see the ad and contact you.

Direct Mail

Direct mail is the technique of sending messages to prospective clients via prepared mailing lists. The advantage of direct mail is that you not only control who reads your ad, but how many direct mail pieces you need to produce.

The main component of a direct mail is a letter that describes a studio's products and services and encourages the reader to act. The design should also enhance the message sent. Before purchasing a mailing list, you should gather some information on the people on the list. What has been the response rate for direct mail? At what rate did respondents buy goods?

You can evaluate the value of direct mail by running limited test mailings. A poorly designed and planned campaign can be expensive, and your studio's direct mail piece can get lost in the vast amounts of junk mail received daily.

Television

Television is only useful if your studio has a wide appeal and you have the ability to pay for the costs of production and airtime. While national TV advertising is often too expensive for start-up studios, advertising on local public-access television can be affordable. The Federal Communications Commission (FCC) has mandated that cable companies must provide one dedicated public access channel in their service area. The advantage of public access TV is that many shows cater to local groups and enthusiasts who would never have a show on mainstream TV.

Point of Sale

Also known as point of purchase (POP) advertising, point of sale is an inexpensive way to advertise your recording studio at the register counter of a retail store. Advertise your recording studio's name and logo on items such as pens, scratch pads, order blanks, or business cards.

Yellow Pages

Customers often look for information in the yellow pages. As with any ad, a yellow pages ad requires some imagination to separate your studio from those around you. The yellow pages staff can assist you with this, as they offer various rates for different ad styles.

Public Relations & Promotion

As noted in the last chapter, public relations is nonpaid information about a recording studio that helps to build an awareness, create a positive image, and persuade people to become customers. Today customers are wary of advertising and the often outlandish statements that it contains. Handled well, public relations can be as effective as advertising and is often cheaper.

Public relations take many forms, which are often not obvious to a company:

- The business culture. The studio's professionalism, appearance, and return policies are important.

- Business brochures that reflect the status and benefits of a recording studio over its nearest competitors. Logos and testimonials are powerful tools in drawing customers.

- Newsletters are a good method of maintaining contact with customers. They can improve the image of a studio through human-interest stories. You can profile a specific customer or highlight positive sales.

- Special events, grand openings, and contests often generate interest from newspapers and customers alike. These events help attract foot traffic to a new business.

- Trade shows are useful in developing relationships with other professionals in the recording industry. These events help expand your business-to-business clientele and build your customer base.

- Speaking engagements on television and radio, and at industry events, colleges, and universities, are useful in finding potential clients.

- Writing articles, columns, and research reports helps to identify you as an expert in a particular area of recording technology.

- Membership in clubs, the chamber of commerce, and professional associations, and getting involved in committees, will also put you in contact with important people in your field.

- Charitable contributions and volunteering give the impression that your recording studio has a social mission within its community. Sponsoring music organizations can achieve the same effect.

- Generating publicity is the most effective method of delivering your studio's information. News releases, public service announcements, and letters to the editor are all valid methods.

Promotion Kits

A promotional kit is an important package distributed to various media that includes the following elements: a cover letter, a brochure about your studio's products and services, a biography, past media coverage, and a CD showing what you actually produce. You can create a different promotion kit for separate products, services, and clients.

Cover Letter

This is your introduction to the reader. Before writing your cover letter you should answer four questions:

- Why are you writing this letter?

- What do you want from the reader?

- What products or services do you offer?

- What do you want your reader to do?

You must write the letter in a professional manner that inspires the reader to open other parts of the kit. It is customary to address the letter to a specific person, rather than an anonymous reader. Your letter should present strong evidence of your recording studio's abilities and success. You can link this information to aspects of your background, such as degrees or diplomas earned. Include information on any awards, well-known clients, and superior performance. Instead of itemizing every detail, choose three or four key examples. At the conclusion, tell readers what they should do: for instance, contact you, read the information package, or set up a meeting.

Brochure

A brochure should explain your services, products, studio equipment, and other relevant information. Base your brochure designs on the amount of information you want to convey and your budget. Folding 8.5- by 11-inch paper into thirds creates a simple version that fits into a business envelope for mailing. Include on the back your return address. The pages inside should include testimonials, benefits, and prices along with the actual services and products provided.

Biography

A well-written biography does more than give a synopsis of a person's life and achievements. It introduces a potential client to a person rather than an impersonal company. A good biography contains information on your education, honors and awards, and experience and shows the reader that you have the ability to complete the tasks in hand. To create interest, your biography needs to develop a hook. Focus on your interests, philosophy, and goals.

Past Media Coverage

The opinions of others can strengthen your promotion kit. Positive reviews or interviews should be included in your promotion kit. Often people read published reviews as impartial information about your studio. If you have not had these yet, include testimonials from satisfied customers.

Promotional CD

The promotional CD should represent what your recording studio does and what it does best. As with other parts of your promotional kit, keep your demo CD to a few examples. Your goal is not to overwhelm the listener. Examples should be no longer than 30 seconds, with some full musical examples toward the end of the CD.

If your studio is involved in a variety of recording projects, you could have a demo for each musical style. For example, if you record jingles, you could create a demo with examples of the jingles that you have created. If you have recorded many heavy metal bands, you could conceivably have a demo for that clientele. Make sure that the examples are consistent in volume levels, tone, and balance. Remember, you want to show potential customers your best work.

Business Card

A business card should be included in your promotional kit. As your calling card it should be simple yet informative, and include your full name and title, studio name and address, telephone and fax numbers, e-mail address, and Web site, if you have created one.

Use a graphic artist to incorporate design elements into the card, such as the studio logo and colors that reflect your packaging.

Press Release

Press releases have a dual function. They allow you to direct the tone of articles written about your business, and they reduce the work a newspaper or promoter needs to do by creating a story about your studio.

Press releases need to be short but descriptive, informative, and interesting. Use your biography as a starting point. The first paragraph should tell the reader who you are, what you do, and where you are located, and the final section may repeat important information such as names of your staff, addresses, and telephone numbers.

Press releases should be double-spaced and on one page, with the business name, address, contact name, and telephone number in the upper left corner. Place the date in the upper right corner. Include a release date (e.g., "For Immediate Release," "For Release after May 24"). If this material is time sensitive you should follow up with a phone call.

Use an interesting headline to catch the attention of the reader. Know your target audience and media, and make sure this news is relevant.

Network and develop a good relationship with the media. This will increase the chances of getting a story covered. You can get better results if you send press releases to a specific department or individual.

Chapter Summary

1. The purpose of advertising is to build an awareness of your studio in potential clients.

2. An adverting budget should be within the scope of the overall studio budget, while still meeting your overall goals.

3. There are eight media vehicles you can use to reach your audience: print (newspapers and magazines), radio, fliers, classified advertising, direct mail, television, point of sale advertising (logo placement on pens, note paper, etc.), and yellow pages.

4. Public relations is nonpaid communication to achieve three objectives: to build awareness of your studio in a target audience, to create a positive image in the public eye, and to inform people about your products and services.

5. A promotional kit is often the best method of sending information to a chosen media. A standard kit consists of the following documents: cover letter, brochure, biography, past media coverage about the studio, promotional CD, business cards, and press release.

12. Legal Issues

After reading this chapter, you should be able to:
- Comprehend basic recording studio contracts.
- File the appropriate copyright applications.
- Understand patent protection.
- File trademark and service mark protection.

This chapter provides an overview of some key issues in contract law and property law. Areas of discussion include contracts, sales laws, warranties, copyright, patents, trademarks, and service marks. Each topic has a direct impact on your recording studio and how it functions. For specific legal advice, you should consult with a qualified attorney in one of the areas mentioned.

Contract Law

Contracts are legal instruments that define an agreement between two or more parties. You will come across contracts in many of your business dealings, including when you buy or sell goods, lease equipment, or enter into an agreement. A contract can be simple or complex, written or oral. However, six essential elements are required for a contract to be valid:

1. Agreement. This is a definite offer communicated to a person and his or her acceptance of the terms.

2. Consent. No contract is enforceable if there is an honest mistake, duress (undue pressure to enter into a contract), or fraud.

3. Capacity. Both parties must be able to enter into a contract. Minors (persons under the legal age, for example 18 or 21) cannot enter into a contract.

4. Consideration. This is the exchange of something of value, such as money or other goods and services.

5. Legality. A contract must conform to all federal, state, and local laws. Two parties can't enter into a contract to sell illegally obtained material.

6. Proper form. The contract must follow certain legal principles governing its form. For example, if the sale of goods exceeds $500, a contract must be in writing.

Since oral contracts are difficult to substantiate in disputes, written contracts are preferred. Whether you write a contract yourself or have an attorney prepare it, a written contract should contain these elements:

1. The names, addresses, and identification (often Social Security numbers) of the parties involved. The contract may include an appointment designation such as power of attorney, which authorizes a person to act as an attorney on your behalf. Power of attorney is useful if one party cannot be present or is not legally able to sign a contract.

2. Contract duration. This section includes the dates by which the contract must be signed, specific duties completed, and payment made. If any party does not fulfill the requirements by the specified date, a contract may be null and void and the person in breach of contract. A record contract, for instance, should last as long as it takes to produce an album. If the need might arise to add tracks or sweeten parts of the album, this needs to be included in the contract.

3. Geographical territory of operation. This indicates in which state the contract has legal authorization—especially important if your clients are from another state.

4. Ownership of material. This part of a contract deals with copyright, trademark, and patent issues.

5. Payment. Here the contract addresses type of payment (for example, up-front payment, percentage payment, barter, or a percentage of future royalties) and timing of payment (at the beginning of the recording session, or on a weekly, monthly, or quarterly basis).

6. Release requirements. This section explains how parties in a contract can end their obligations.

7. Cost coverage. This clause should also clearly indicate if any taxes will be withheld or need to be paid.

8. Breach of contract remedies and arbitration. This clause deals with legal disputes and the means of resolution. In most cases, the parties opt for judgment in a court of law or through arbitration, which is the procedure of handling conflicts without litigation. Often groups rely on the American Association of Arbitrators to provide them with a list of organizations that carry out arbitration. Depending on the wording of this clause and the state in which the arbitration takes place, an arbitration may not be open to appeal.

9. Termination or expiration of contract. This contract clause comes into operation when one party has not fulfilled the requirements as set out in the previous sections. This clause should include information on what will happen to a recording or master if

there is a termination. Known as the force majeure or "act of God" clause, it allows termination of a contract under circumstances beyond the control of the parties, including weather-related events or natural disasters.

10. Mode of contract. This clause specifies how the parties will deal with each other, and which signatories are required. If your studio has an attorney, a client may need to deal with your attorney rather than directly with you.

11. Signatures of parties and witnesses. These should be dated and include identification. Witnesses, such justices of the peace, give validation to a contract but are often not necessary.

Property Law

Property law covers the transfer of property from one party to another, and the laws governing it are complex. There are four definitions of property:

1. Tangible real property. This includes land and anything attached on it such as houses, factories, or warehouses.

2. Tangible personal property. Any moving object with a physical existence, such as cars, sound equipment, or CDs.

3. Intangible personal property. Anything that has no physical existence but exists in the form of a written document. Examples include bank accounts, stocks, and customer lists.

4. Intellectual property. Property formed from the production of human knowledge, discovery, invention, and creativity.

The final definition of property has the greatest impact on the operation of a recording studio. Songs, recordings, books, and software are all examples of intellectual property created from your studio. As such, there are several forms of legal protection for your creations or those of your clients. These include copyrights, patents, trademarks, and service marks.

Copyright

Copyright is the ownership of dramatic, musical, artistic, scientific, and other intellectual works. A copyright gives the owner of a recording, for instance, the exclusive right to reproduce (copy), sell, or modify the work. Furthermore, a copyright protects its owner from others using the material without permission.

To be copyrighted, a recording or some other artistic work must fulfill certain criteria:

1. Fixation. The work must be in a tangible medium of expression. It can be written (such as in a book or in sheet music) or recorded (such as on CD, tape, or DAT).

2. Originality. The work must be original. It cannot be someone else's work or it would violate copyright law.

There are certain legal rights associated with copyright ownership:

1. Reproduction of a work.

2. Preparation of derivative works.

3. Public distribution of a copyrighted work.

4. Public performance of a copyrighted work.

.5 Digital performance of a sound recording, such as the performance of an MP3 file on your computer.

Registration

Registration does not affect the existence of a copyright. You can claim copyright on a work if it is in a tangible form, even if you have not registered the copyright. However, registering a work is important for three reasons:

- It is a prerequisite for bringing a suit to enforce a copyright.

- Registration creates the right to receive compensation for any infringement. In general, you cannot recover attorney fees or so-called statutory damages for any infringement that commences before the "effective date," or registration.

- If you are the owner of copyright in a musical work, you are not entitled to royalties under a compulsory license until your identity is a matter of record with the Copyright Office.

Applications for registration in the United States are handled by the Copyright Office. The application process has three components: filing the registration form, paying the deposit, and placing copyright notification on your property.

The type of form used for copyright protection depends on the type and function of the work. Here are some of the key forms that you may use in your recording studio:

- Form TX. Use this form for a nondramatic literary work other than a periodical or serial work. (Form SE is appropriate for journals.)

- Form PA. Used for a dramatic work or any other work of the performing arts (including music, dance, and film). For multimedia works, use form PA if there is any audiovisual component.

- Form SR. This form covers all sound recordings. If you record the works of a single composer, the SR form can be used without an accompanying PA form.

- Form CA. This form is for correcting anything you sent previously.

All forms are available from the information and publications section of the Copyright Office, and can be downloaded at www.copyright.gov. Registration forms require certain basic information:

- The name and address of the person filing the copyright.

- The name of the author(s), unless the work is published anonymously or under a pseudonym, and a brief description of each author's contribution to the work. This is important if there is a clear delineation between the lyricist and composer.

- If one or more of the authors is dead, the dates of their deaths.

- If the copyright claimant is someone other than the author(s), a brief statement of how the claimant came by the copyright (for example, "written transfer of copyright").

- If the work is a compilation, a statement identifying the pre-existing work or works that it incorporates. If the composition is a derivative work, a statement identifying the work or works on which it is based. The document should also identify what material is original. This can be a simple statement such as "substantially revised and updated text."

- The title of the work. If the work had any other titles, such as a song published outside the country, those titles should be included.

- The year in which "creation of the work was completed." This should be the year of completion in its final form. If there are substantial changes to a work, the author may be entitled to copyright the work as a new composition.

- If the work has been published, the first date of publication.

Deposit

Either one or two copies of the work, plus a $35 fee, must accompany the deposit of an application to the Copyright Office. For a published work send two complete copies. If your work is unpublished, you only need to send one copy.

For published works, you need to send examples that are the "best edition." This means recordings should be on a compact disc stereophonically recorded.

Copyright Notice

When your application for registration is approved, the Copyright Office issues you a certificate of registration or a certificate of supplementary registration. It is then up to you to place a copyright notice on your material. A notice of copyright has three elements:

1. The familiar symbol ©, or if you prefer the word *copyright* or its accepted abbreviation, *Copr.* (If you plan to sell goods in foreign

Things That You Cannot Copyright

The law is very clear in what you cannot copyright:

1. Trivial matters, such as titles, slogans, and names (there are other means for protecting these).

2. Ideas. You can protect the expression of an idea, but not the idea itself.

3. Utilitarian objects. These are things that produce other things. For example, you cannot file for copyright protection for a lamp, because the production of light is a utilitarian function. The *design* of a lamp can be protected.

4. Formulas, equations, methods, or systems. Again, you cannot grant a copyright to an idea, but you can protect the description or explanation of that idea.

countries use ©, since *Copyright* and *Copr.* don't have international validity. In the case of a sound recording use the symbol Ⓟ; © is of no effect.)

2. The year of first publication. The year of first publication of a work may not necessarily be the year in which you first need to affix a copyright notice. For example, a recording is considered to be published on the date of distribution, not creation.

3. The name of the owner of copyright. An abbreviated version of the name can be used, as long as the original name remains recognizable. If the owner has a generally known trademark, abbreviation, or other symbol, that may be used.

Place these symbols in areas that are permanently legible to the user. Several areas are acceptable on a compact disc: the back panel of the jewel case, the last page of the booklet, or on the compact disc itself.

Patents

A patent is a legal protection that gives an inventor the right to make, use, or sell an invention for 20 years. For a patent to be protected it must be clearly different from any other invention, be a working object (ideas are not acceptable), and not be something obvious to people working in a field.

Filing a patent is a long and expensive undertaking. A recording studio interested in protecting an invention must file a disclosure document with the U.S. Patent and Trademark Office that describes the creation in writings or drawings. This establishes the date of origin for the invention and will remain confidential for two years, allowing you to complete work on the patent application.

The next step is a patent search, which establishes the originality of an invention. This is a time-consuming and expensive process, often handled by a patent lawyer. At this stage, it is essential that you prove no registration exists for a similar invention.

Once you have established that your invention can be patented, your next step is to file an application form with the Patent and Trademark Office. An application consists of eight parts:

1. An abstract.

2. Specifications.

3. Proof of the invention's originality.

4. Declaration stating that the invention is original and you are the inventor.

5. Drawings of the invention.

6. The application fee.

7. A self-addressed, stamped envelope, so the Patent Office can inform you that the application is being processed.

Maintaining a patent requires you to pay regular registration fees as well as marking your patent with the appropriate numbering. Furthermore, you are responsible for the protection of your patent and the litigation of infringers.

Trademarks & Service Marks

A trademark is a word, phrase, logo, or graphic symbol used to distinguish a company's products from those of its competitors. Trademarks are identified by the symbol ™ placed on the product.

A service mark, indicated by the ˢᴹ symbol, is a name or logo that identifies a service offered to customers. For example, if you only intend to record your clients' music, your studio is only providing a service, not a product. The symbol ® indicates that you have received federal trademark protection from the Patent and Trademark Office.

The most important aspect of filing a trademark or service mark is to start a name search. If no company uses a particular name, you need to first file with the appropriate state office. If you use a mark across state, territorial, or national lines, register it with the U.S. Patent and Trademark Office.

Chapter Summary

1. A contract is a legally binding agreement between two or more parties. Both written and oral contracts require that: there is an agreement between the parties; both parties consent to the contract; both parties are legally able to enter into a contract; something of value has been exchanged; the contract is legal; and the contract is in proper form.

2. Copyright is the ownership of dramatic, musical, artistic, and other intellectual works. Two factors that must be present to grant copyright are fixation in a tangible form and originality. The U.S. Copyright Office handles copyright registration.

3. Patents are the legal protection of inventions and are filed with the U.S. Patent and Trademark Office.

4. A trademark is the protection of a word, phrase, logo, or other graphic symbol. Service marks are used to identify services offered to customers. The U.S. Patent and Trademark Office handles registration of trademarks and service marks.

13. Bookkeeping & Taxes

After reading this chapter, you should be able to:
- Prepare various financial statements for your studio.
- Keep records of your cash disbursements.
- Understand the principles of income, sales, property, and inventory tax.

Accurate and complete bookkeeping is an important part of any business. Several government agencies and private investors regularly assess financial records, including the IRS, state income taxation authorities, the Federal Trade Commission, and banks. Since you have to prove to these agencies, especially the IRS, that your studio is a legitimate business and not a hobby, you need to develop an efficient bookkeeping system that documents and organizes all transactions.

You can handle simple transactions through a business checking account. Keep this account solely for business transactions, not for personal use. For sales, use an invoice receipt system with consecutive numbers. For payments, use the checkbook as often as possible. If you must use cash, get a receipt of the transaction for future record.

Credit cards are another effective and simple way to record transactions. Just remember not to exceed your credit limit and to avoid carrying a balance if you can.

A checking account gives you what is called a single-entry accounting system. The system is simple and may be sufficient for a beginning studio, but is often fraught with error. Make sure that you state the amount that you started with, what you put into the account, and what went out. Balance the account at the end of a period. If you keep track of everything correctly, an accountant should be able to prepare accurate tax returns and financial statements.

Double-entry bookkeeping is the most accurate system. In this accounting system every transaction is entered as a debit and a corresponding credit. Since every debit has a corresponding credit entry, the ledger should balance out. This system allows for accrual basis accounting, which expresses expenses even if they are not paid. This is the generally accepted accounting method that all public companies must use for reporting. Double-entry bookkeeping also allows for the preparation of cash flow statements, balance sheets, and income statements. You can use it to maintain current receivable and payable balances.

General Financial Records

Businesses commonly use financial records that track daily, monthly, quarterly, and yearly transactions, which are the basis for tax payment. This information also helps you analyze financial trends and implement changes during the life of your recording studio. We will discuss the most common financial records in use.

Revenue & Expense Journal

A revenue and expense journal keeps a record of individual transactions over a period of time. Record the transactions as revenues (sales and interest) or expenses (payments for products and services). At the end of a month, calculate the totals. The results from this journal will form the basis of a profit and loss statement.

Accounts Payable

This is a record of debts owed by your recording studio—how much you owe and when it is due. This information is important, since late payment affects your credit rating and therefore your ability to borrow money.

Accounts Receivable

This is a record of debts owed to your recording studio. Each customer should have a separate page with the details of balances due and previous payment history. At the end of each month, your customers should receive a statement of balance.

Fixed Assets

This is a list of all your studio's tangible and intangible assets. It also includes assets that you purchased for your studio, are not for resale, and have been capitalized or depreciated over a specific number of years. Examples include buildings, office equipment, and production equipment. These items are often tax deductible. Since tax regulations on depreciation are complex, it is wise to consult with your tax preparer on this matter.

Petty Cash Record

This is a list of all purchases made with cash or personal checks. You should pay a deposit in the petty cash record with a business check and record it as an expense in your revenue and expense journal.

Inventory Record

Even if you are only recording music and therefore are acting as a service business, it is a good idea to have an inventory control system as part of your bookkeeping. This ledger records all the products purchased or manufactured for resale. An inventory record is also a powerful tool for ordering and controlling purchases. A well-maintained inventory list shows which items sold well, when your studio should order more material, and the minimum amount of inventory your studio needs to operate, thus saving money on overspending.

Payroll

Payroll records are extremely important and are subject to some of the most complicated tax laws. The IRS has strict regulations regarding payroll, and failure to comply with these laws can result in heavy fines. The best thing to do is to leave these records to a trained tax expert. (See chapter 16 for information on employee taxes.)

Controlling Cash

To operate your studio in the most efficient manner, you must manage your cash effectively. To control your studio's cash receipts, you can do three things:

- Require full payment or partial payment up front (you may need to offer some incentive to your customer).
- Charge late fees and interest for defaulted payment.
- Deposit all cash and checks promptly in your interest-bearing account.

Similarly, you can give your studio some extra cash by controlling cash disbursements. These methods help you control your payments:

- Lease rather than buy.
- If you can pay with cash, ask for a discount.
- Don't pay your bills too far in advance, unless there is an incentive.
- Use credit cards to give you time to earn money.
- Avoid unnecessary purchases.
- Ask for discounts.
- Use non-cash and non-income forms of employee compensation.

Tax Basics

As the wise saying goes, the only two certainties in life are death and taxes, so a recording studio owner must pay taxes on a regular basis. Whether they are federal, state, or local taxes, they can take a big chunk out of your profits and out of your time as you spend long, frustrating hours trying to unravel the complexities of tax law. That it is why it is imperative that you hire a qualified accountant who can help you through taxes and allow you to concentrate on creating music. Even so, understanding the basics of tax law and collection will help you plan and react to any changes.

The first important tax requirement is that you identify yourself to the Internal Revenue Service. The IRS will recognize you and your recording studio based on your Social Security number or employer identification number (EIN), a nine-digit number issued by

Federal Corporate Income Tax Rates

Amount	Taxable Income
$0 to $50,000	15%
$50,000 to $75,000	25%
$75,000 to $100,000	34%
$100,000 to $335,000	39%
$335,000 to $10,000,000	34%
$10,000,000 to $15,000,000	35%
$15,000,000 to $18,333,333	38%
Over $18,333,3333	35%

An S corporation does not bear any federal income tax at the corporate level. Since an S corporation passes income directly to the shareholder, its distributive share of the corporation's income or loss is taxable.

the IRS. If you own a corporation or a partnership or have employees (employee tax is covered in chapter 16), you will need an EIN number. You can obtain an EIN number by filing an SS-4 application with the IRS.

Your business structure has the greatest influence on the type of tax you will pay. Taxation for corporations occurs twice. Taxation for sole proprietorships, partnerships, and limited liability companies occurs once on earnings.

If you own a sole proprietorship, the IRS requires that you file a Schedule C (Profit or Loss from a Business or Profession) with form 1040. Although sole proprietors do not pay unemployment taxes for themselves, which is an advantage over the other business forms, they may be required to provide retirement plans for any employees. Furthermore, there are no federal tax breaks for the cost of group term life, medical, and disability insurance coverage.

For a partnership, each partner must include a statement of the partnership's distribution, income, losses, deductions, and/or credits on his or her federal income tax (form 1040). Since the partners' cash income is not a salary, there is no tax withholding at the source, and each partner must pay self-employment taxes as if he or she were a sole proprietor. As with a sole proprietorship, partnerships do not pay unemployment tax; and since there is no income tax withheld, estimated payments are paid quarterly for federal and state taxes.

Corporations must file both federal and state taxes. Tax payment varies depending on the type of corporation (S corporation, C corporation). A corporation is subject to federal income tax on its earnings. If the corporation distributes earnings to shareholders as dividends, both the shareholder and corporation pay tax on them. This still holds true if the corporation distributes all its earnings to shareholders upon liquidation. If the corporation decides not to distribute the dividends and opts for the corporate accumulated-earnings tax, it may end up paying an amount equal to the highest individual tax rate imposed on single-return filers. (See the table for corporate tax rates.)

Other taxes paid by corporations include:

- Federal taxes, including Social Security tax.

- Federal unemployment tax, income withholding, and business income tax.

- State taxes, including income withholding, sales/use taxes, and business income.
- Local taxes, usually including property tax, city income tax, and economic development tax.
- Inventory tax.

Sales Tax

Sales and property taxes vary from state to state, and some cities even have their own tax rate. Certain businesses incur greater tax and fee burdens than others do. In most states that require sales tax, you must file for a license or permit before you can commence your business. Most businesses pay monthly or quarterly estimated or actual sales tax, depending on volume and amount owed.

If you sell your goods in another state, you may need to collect a sales tax from that state. Keep your accountant informed of any such transactions. Currently, sales tax is exempt on the Internet for items bought interstate. For information about sales tax or obtaining a permit, contact your state tax department.

Property Tax

If you own your own property, you owe property tax to your county or township assessor's office. This is collected either yearly or twice a year and is sometimes paid through a mortgage.

Inventory Tax

This is a tax on inventory you own in your factory or warehouse. This is usually an annual state tax, and many states are doing away with it.

Tax Deductions

The IRS understands that running a recording studio, or any other business, can be an expensive undertaking. To alleviate some of the burden, the IRS allows certain deductions to be factored into tax payment. According to the IRS, a deduction must be "ordinary and necessary." Ordinary expenses are those that are common to your field, and necessary expenses help you complete the job. In general, there are six expense categories on which you can claim deductions: equipment, automobile, business, meals and entertainment, home office, and travel.

Equipment

Recording studio equipment is often expensive and must be repaired and replaced on a regular basis. The government has two methods for claiming a deduction for equipment.

1. You can claim depreciation for the equipment over a period of several years.
2. You can deduct the full cost of the equipment purchased, by filing section 179 (expensing allowance). Originally you could deduct up to $25,000, but in 2003 the Jobs and Growth Tax Relief Act increased that amount to $100,000.

Automobile

If you use your car for business, the IRS allows you to deduct related expenses from your tax. As with equipment deductions, you can deduct the cost of your vehicle in two ways:

1. You can keep track of actual business-related expenses, including depreciation, gas, insurance, leasing fees, repairs, and tolls. If you use this method, you must keep all of your receipts. The deduction allowed is calculated by multiplying the total costs by the total mileage traveled for business.

2. You can claim the standard IRS mileage rate. This is a specific amount you can deduct for each mile, which is adjusted on an annual basis. You can use this system in the first year that you use your car for business. After that year, you can use either the mileage rate or actual expenses for one car, or the actual expenses if you claim two or more vehicles.

Business

Business deductions can help you reduce your tax burden considerably. Some of the most common deductions are:

- Advertising/marketing costs.
- Postage.
- Telephone answering services.
- Utilities.
- Employee wages.
- Legal fees.
- Online information services.
- Delivery services.
- Business stationery.
- Office supplies.
- Membership dues to professional organizations.
- Recording publications.

As with all deductions, it is important for you to keep records and receipts to verify actual payment.

Meals & Entertainment

A percentage of business meals and entertainment can be deducted from your tax. However, meals must fall within the parameters of deductibility set by the IRS. The expense must be ordinary, not lavish, and you must show that the meal was essential for conducting business or came after substantial business discussion. It is important to keep records of the amount spent (especially if the meal cost more than $75), date, location, type of entertainment, name, and occupation of the people that you entertained.

Home Office

If you structured your recording studio as a sole proprietor and you operate out of your home, you may be eligible for a deduction on your home office. To claim a deduction, your home must be your primary place of business; you cannot claim your home as a business deduction if you have an outside office as well. This is one deduction that IRS scrutinizes very closely, so before claiming your home as a deduction, consult your accountant.

Travel

You can deduct travel expenses when you are away from your home on business. Items that can be deducted include transportation, accommodation, and meals. Keep records also of telephone calls and faxes, as they are considered a travel deduction.

Chapter Summary

1. Accurate bookkeeping is important for a recording studio. Double-entry bookkeeping is the generally accepted accounting method among government agencies and most industries.

2. Financial records help you with financial and tax planning. These documents cover areas such as your studio's accounts receivable and payable, assets, revenue and expenses, and payroll.

3. Cash is king in business. Controlling it helps you run your studio efficiently and effectively.

4. The amount a recording studio pays in income and corporate tax is based on its business structure. A studio may also face sales tax (depending on the state in which the studio is located), property tax (if you own property), and inventory tax.

5. As a business owner, you can substantially reduce your tax burden through deductions. There are six basic expense categories on which you can claim deductions: equipment, automobile, business, meals and entertainment, home office, and travel.

14. Recording Practices

After reading this chapter, you should be able to:

- Create a thorough preproduction plan for placement of performers and mics.
- Utilize mic techniques and gobos to help isolate sounds and reduce comb filtering.
- Use EQ during tracking to sculpt a great sound that inspires performers.
- Solve noise, interference, and tonal issues with parametric EQ and other tools.
- Understand and translate audio jargon into specific technical and artistic tasks.
- Make the most effective use of digital levels and proper headroom.

The topic of recording practices is a mammoth one, much too large to be tackled completely here. Entire books could be dedicated to just portions of the subject matter, and indeed many have been. Instead of trying to be encyclopedic, this chapter offers useful advice regarding some fundamental, yet often overlooked, practical aspects of recording and mixing. The first two sections cover preproduction and tracking concepts, while the final section offers a few additional tips for success in the studio.

Room Placement

Room placement decisions are fundamental to the making of a good recording, and yet they are often given little thought. Many times they are left to the last moment, when the musicians begin loading in their gear. Sometimes engineers just let the musicians set up without considering the best locations for acoustics, mic placement, and performance.

Some believe that microphone choice and placement cover all sins, while others, working in budget-oriented studios, may think that such considerations make no difference in their poorly devised acoustic spaces. Neither could be further from the truth. Well-orchestrated room placement is key to the smooth running of any tracking session. It creates a comfortable environment for the musicians (which is more likely to yield good performances), better tone, and a clear final mix. A solid preset plan for the specific instruments of a tracking session is essential and should be completed well before setup begins—even before the day of the first session.

Work on a plan that will produce the best possible recording, specific to the space and the resources on hand. Don't be misled by industry propaganda: Having the best gear and the perfect room is no guarantee of that you'll achieve great tone. In fact, many great recordings have been made on mediocre equipment in less than ideal acoustical environments. It is the knowledge, skill, planning, and creativity of the engineer (along with some help from talented musicians and producers) that makes fantastic recordings possible under any circumstances.

Working with limitations can sometimes be a bit frightening, particularly in home-based studios. This becomes especially evident when a five-piece rock group wants to track everyone simultaneously in your basement. Regardless of the circumstances, however, by applying a few fundamental room placement and session analysis techniques to create a session plan, you can greatly improve the chances of success.

Again, all planning must be done before the session takes place. A preproduction meeting with the clients is a must to gather information regarding the exact personnel and equipment. They should also bring example recordings of themselves or other artists whose recordings and music they admire. These can help start a dialogue about the particular types of recorded sounds they are looking for. It also improves your client relationship, helping them feel you are as dedicated to the project as they are. Advance planning will also keep questions like "Where should I put the drums?" to a minimum, keep unpleasant surprises at bay, and allow everyone to focus more time on performance.

The four key concepts of room placement are talent comfort, line of sight, isolation between instruments, and room acoustics. When planning your room placement for a specific session, these four concerns should generally be addressed in the same order. In some instances, you may need to consider room acoustics first, but only to inform decisions regarding talent comfort, line of sight, and isolation, not to supercede them. Inevitably, however, compromises are necessary.

Talent Comfort

Talent comfort primarily means having enough physical space to house the instrument, performer, and all other members of the group in a way that won't feel cramped or hamper their creativity. If the musicians are comfortable in the studio, they will deliver better performances overall. Drum kits, for instance, can take up a lot of space. You should set aside enough space for the physical size of the kit, for the musicians to move around, for easy access to all drums by the engineer, and for all the mics and stands required.

Comfort is about more than physical space in the tracking room, however. Be sure the musicians (and any producers or managers around) have a nice supply of cold bottled water. A separate table for these (plus headphones, ashtray, paper, pens, or anything else the talent might need) should be located within the room. This will avoid long breaks between takes spent looking for water or cleaning up spilled items.

Let's use the bass player as an example. Does he want to stand or sit? Does he move around a lot, or does he prefer to stand next to the drummer and feel the kick drum while playing? In most cases, it's best to set up the musicians similarly to how they rehearse. Forcing them to do something different in a session may lead to grumpy, dissatisfied clients and bad performances.

On all instruments connected to amplifiers, the setups should allow easy access to controls for adjustment and tuning purposes. Performers should tune at the start of each take, and it goes a lot quicker when they can put their amp on standby, unplug, and then tune. A studio tuner with a fresh supply of batteries is a must.

Locating amplifiers close to the performers is also convenient for headphone cue mixing while tracking. If they cannot hear themselves well enough, instead of asking you to turn up their headphones, they can just move closer to their amplifiers (a move they are used to making live).

Just put yourself in the players' shoes and think about what needs they might have. If you're ever unsure, you can always just ask.

Line of Sight

Performers and instruments should be placed in a way that everyone can see each other. Think about their situation: They are performing in an environment they have never played in before, they are not used to wearing headphones, and they feel pressure to deliver one of their best performances. And you expect them to do so when they can't even see each other?

If you look at most rehearsal setups, the musicians are gathered in a circle, close to each other. This allows for visual cues, anticipation for the next part of the song, and overall better communication during the tune. When thinking about room placement, try to create a similar dynamic.

In addition to seeing each other, most of the group members should be able to see the engineer. While not always possible, this eye contact helps tremendously during overdubs and in the start and stop points of a song. It also aids in overall better communication during the tracking session and allows the engineer to see if anything in the setup has moved accidentally. When creating a line of sight, keep in mind that the guitar player can turn in any direction while playing. You can point the amp however you like, regardless of which way the guitarist is facing. On the other hand, drums, horns, vocals, and keys are a lot more stationary and must be placed in the direction of line of sight. Good placement helps the talent function as a group, producing a tighter, more confident performance.

Isolation

Isolation is often what beginning engineers consider first when dealing with room placement. A better line of sight and comfortable talent, however, always yield better recordings than if everything is isolated but the performers cannot express themselves well. Isolation is important, but you have to make sure the musicians can play well before you focus on the more technical aspects of the recording.

The idea behind sonic isolation is to create enough separation between instruments so that the mic on one sound source does not pick up too much of the sound of the other instruments. This is crucial when it's time to mix the song. If there is too much sound from one instrument picked up by another mic (a problem known as bleed), then you have less control of their relative balance in the mix and their placement in the stereo field. Bleed also increases the chance of phase problems and comb filtering.

For example, if there is strong bleed from the guitar amp into the drum overhead mics, when the cymbals are brought up in the mix, the guitar also becomes louder. When the band does overdubs and multiple takes, it's impossible to entirely get rid of older tracks if they have bled over to other instrumental (or vocal) takes you want to keep. In cases like this you'll hear ghosts of the previous unwanted takes that you cannot remove.

Smart mic placement deals with the direction in which the source is projecting in the room. If there is too much bleed from the bass amp into the kick drum mic, you may correct it by pointing the bass amp away from the drum set. Creating a map of performer positions in the studio, the directionality of the sound of their instruments, and the directionality of the microphones can help you avoid many bleed problems.

Sometimes when the room is physically too small and the acoustics are poor, bleed is everywhere and hard to avoid by mic/performer placement combinations. This is a common problem in smaller home-based studios. In such a case, it is often necessary to add extra absorptive (or sometimes reflective) surfaces in specific locations relative to problem mics or sound sources. In essence, you are slightly modifying the room acoustics.

One way to accomplish this is by using rugs, blankets, or specialized movable surfaces called gobos (see chapter 7 for an in-depth description). The basic concepts behind gobo placement are simple. You can use them to surround a sound source and isolate its sound. They can also be placed in the path of reflections to avoid interference issues with the direct sound, or placed between a mic and a secondary source to keep leakage down.

On drums, for example, you could place two large gobos behind the drummer to reduce reflections from the wall behind, or place three small gobos around the front of the drummer to help stop leakage of the kick and snare into other instruments.

To keep vocals from picking up too much of the room sound or losing its presence, you can create a temporary mini-booth with three large gobos to encompass the sides and back of the vocalist. You could use four during solo takes and overdubs. When placing gobos, keep in mind the line of sight issues discussed above.

There are many possible uses and configurations for gobos and other moveable treatments. To use them effectively, just keep basic acoustic principles in mind and be creative.

Room Acoustics

Small studios are notorious for poor design and bad acoustics. Many common problems arise from the use of smaller spaces with low ceilings and highly reflective parallel surfaces. Room modes and reflections are often too strong and create sonic mayhem. These issues are not limited to smaller studios, however, and can happen anywhere. When facing these acoustic problems, a little common sense and listening go a long way.

When planning a session, it's a good idea to get to know the acoustic properties of the rooms. Begin by walking around each space while talking or clapping to energize the room. Listen for acoustically dead areas as well as echoes, modes, and strong reflections.

Next, analyze which instruments will benefit from each area of the room. Drums, because of their acoustic nature, tend to like areas that are more live. Guitar amps, bass amps, and vocals, which are close miked, loud, and produce a more directional sound path, tend to like the areas that are deader. Of course, these sorts of considerations are also a matter of taste and musical style. Bear in mind the particular project's sonic goals when considering options.

Each area of the room can be modified to suit the needs of each instrument. You can adjust miking distances, polar patterns, and angles to find the proper sound. Gobos, blankets, or throw rugs can be used to control reflections and leakage and improve isolation. Listen carefully to the results in the control room, and don't be afraid to reconsider and make changes. It's all about getting the right sound.

After a while you will discover setups you like for each type of recording project. It takes some time to get to know your room. In the meantime, don't get stuck in the mentality of "Drums go there!" just because they look like they should. Keep experimenting. There's always room for improvement.

EQ & Tracking

Once you've placed the performers and instruments and set up mics and gobos, the tonal quality or clarity you're looking for may still be eluding you. This is where EQ comes in.

The technique of adding EQ before tracking (recording) is traditionally known as EQ-ing to tape. This means that the tone achieved with the EQ is captured on the tracks and therefore cannot be undone. Even though this approach may seem risky, if done right, it offers great benefits during both tracking and initial playback. When you do a thorough and proper job of adding EQ before the first take, the performers are inspired to play better. And when the musicians come into the control room to listen to the initial playback, the tune already sounds good even before any real mixing has begun! The excitement that ensues energizes the rest of the project.

In today's digital audio software realm, though, true EQ-ing to tape is rare and unnecessary. In fact, most DAW software uses nondestructive EQ plug-ins that perform the EQ on the outputs after the "tape" (now known as a hard drive). The sonic benefits are the same, but the EQ settings can be changed later if needed.

Many recording engineers use a "fix it in the mix" approach, waiting until mixing to add EQ or compression. The problem with leaving EQ until then is that you are not even sure if your target tone is achievable with EQ until after the recording phase is done. By that point it is too late to use gobos, reconsider mic choice or placement, and adjust or swap out the instrument.

Diagnosing Tonal Problems

To determine the cause of tonal problems, first pan everything to the stereo center position. Next, listen to the offending sound in two ways: in context of the mix, and soloed by itself.

If tonal problems are evident within the context of the mix but disappear when the channel is heard separately, then you're most likely dealing with interference between the mics. If the problems are roughly the same regardless of which listening method you use, then the tone on the channel itself needs some work.

Interference

Let's start by addressing the first problem: interference between two or more microphone channels. Start by soloing the channels one at a time. Listen for a strong presence of the instrument in question, and take note of all the channels that carry this sound. Determine if they are all necessary or if you have gone overboard with miking. Sometimes, simply muting an unnecessary channel is enough to fix an interference problem.

Phase & Delay Methods

Before even touching the EQ, you might try two other techniques. First, invert the phase of the offending sound and listen to it in context. If it is not noticeably better, revert to the original phase.

The next trick has really come into its own in the digital audio/computer age. The idea is to delay the offending track until the combined sound in the mix clears up. This delay is generally anywhere from 1 sample to 9 milliseconds in length. If you find that the best delay time is longer than 2.5 milliseconds, however, you may want to just use the EQ for now and reconsider the delay idea after tracking is done. This is because a delay of this magnitude may begin to throw off the feel of the music for the performers and inhibit their playing.

You can find the appropriate delay time in three ways:

1. Listen while adjusting. This can be quite difficult until your hearing is well trained by experience, but it's probably the best method since the ear will ultimately be the judge.

2. Measure the distance between main mic and those that are causing the interference. Divide the speed of sound by this number, or multiply the number of inches by .0739 (.0291 if using centimeters) to get the total number of milliseconds.

3. Measure the delay. If you record a short burst of sound from the instrument in question into a DAW, you can use the software view and zoom functions to measure the time differences between the channels. This method is usually the most precise but is not guaranteed to uncover the problem.

Equalization Methods

Once you've properly thought through the phase and delay techniques, it is time to go ahead and try some EQ to manage persistent interference problems.

The first approach to consider is removing unnecessary frequency areas from selected channels. A highpass filter can be used to remove lows from the hi-hats or drum overhead microphones (used mainly to pick up cymbals). If a noticeable amount of kick drum is getting into the overhead microphones, it can create phase problems between the kick and the overhead channels because they each pick up the same sound source but at different distances. Of course, this same problem will also affect the mix since every time you raise the cymbal channels, the kick level will be raised too. So the highpass filter solves two problems at once.

Similarly, a lowpass filter might be used to remove highs from the kick drum mic, low toms, or bass. Unnecessary frequencies and sonic energy can reduce clarity in the mix as well as cause drastic shifts in tonal color due to interference. For similar reasons, it is a good idea to mute channels during mixdown when they are not being used or when that instrument is not playing during the arrangement.

A more specific, selective method must be used for mid-frequency issues or when problem areas are too close to the frequency content of the actual instrument. This method is sometimes called the seek and destroy or, for the less violent among us, the search and rescue (the former would refer to cutting frequencies, I suppose, and the latter for boosting frequencies). To perform this you need a high-quality, fully parametric EQ with a wide-range frequency selector.

A snare drum provides a good illustration of how you might use this technique. A common problem with snares is a ring or "poing" sound with a very specific pitch. You can sometimes even hum the note. In some styles, this is exactly the sound desired...but for others, it is definitely not! If tuning or mic placement does not remove this unwanted quality, then it's up to the EQ. Use a midrange parametric with a fairly small bandwidth and turn the gain up high (+12dB or more). Slowly sweep the frequency from 450 to 3,000Hz. At some point the nasty "poing" will leap out with a vengeance. Stop! Leave that frequency setting as it is. You have now completed the search, and now it's time to destroy! By turning the gain back down, now into the negative settings, you can blow that "poing" right out of the water.

Tonal Character

Besides dealing with various forms of interference or noise issues, EQ can be used to sculpt the tonal character of sounds. For example, close-miked vocalists often exhibit what some refer to as a nasal quality. This sounds a little like they are pinching their noses while singing. Once you've determined that there is no ill-placed clothespin and the singer does not have a terrible head cold, it's EQ to the rescue. Due to both mic placement and a bit of proximity effect, this nasal sound is actually due to an exaggeration of frequencies around 300 to 400Hz. Setting a notch filter to this area and slowly bringing the gain down into the negatives will begin to correct the sound.

So far, all EQ mentioned has been used to remove, or cut, frequency areas. However, boosting can also be extremely effective in the right circumstances. Sticking with the vocal example, let's say that the complaint is that the sound is a bit dull. You might fix this by either bringing up the presence somewhere between 1.5 and 4kHz or accentuating the air/brilliance of 8kHz and up. Since the terminology used to describe these various sound qualities is so subjective, it is up to you as the engineer to translate it into probable technical meanings. Try a fix and if it doesn't work, try another.

The following chart was supplied by Bernie Mack, a Chicago-based recording engineer. It is intended to give some ideas from which to start translating client speak (listed under "Goal") into EQ approaches for various instruments. Since this is not a precise science, use the chart as a rough guide only.

Problem-Solving with EQ

Instrument	Goal	Frequency	Cut or Boost
Kick drum	More low-end power/thud	60Hz–80Hz	Boost
	Less boxy/tighter	350Hz–400Hz	Cut
	More slap/beater attack	5kHz–7kHz	Boost
Snare	Less hi-hat bleed in channel	300Hz–350Hz	Cut
	More snap/whack	2kHz–5kHz	Boost
	More snare wire definition	10kHz–12kHz	Boost
Toms	More low-end power/thud	60Hz–80Hz	Boost
	Less boxy/tighter	350Hz–400Hz	Cut
	More stick attack	4kHz–5kHz	Boost
Hi-hat	Less kick bleed in channel	60Hz–80Hz	Cut
	Less "garbage can lid"	300Hz–400Hz	Cut
	More clarity on stick hit	10kHz–12kHz	Boost
Overhead mic right over cymbal	Less kick bleed in channel	60Hz–100Hz	Cut
	Less kit bleed in channel	250Hz–350Hz	Cut
Bass guitar with amp	More low end	60Hz–80Hz	Boost
	Less space taken up in mix by low end	100Hz–120Hz	Cut
	More warmth	250Hz–300Hz	Boost
	More string attack/definition	3kHz–7kHz	Boost
Electric guitar, overdriven/distorted with amp	Less conflict with bass guitar in mix	50Hz–60Hz	Cut
	More warmth	200Hz–250Hz	Boost
	More clarity on individual notes	7kHz–10kHz	Boost
Electric guitar, clean with amp	Less conflict with bass guitar	60Hz–80Hz	Cut
	More warmth	200Hz–250Hz	Boost
	More clarity on individual notes	7kHz–10kHz	Boost

Instrument	Goal	Frequency	Cut or Boost
Keyboards, direct	Less muddy	200Hz–250Hz	Cut
	More attack on individual notes	5kHz–7kHz	Boost
Brass horns	More body/bell	300Hz–350Hz	Boost
	More bite/bright	5kHz–7kHz	Boost
Banjo	More tambourine/percussive	200Hz–250Hz	Boost
	More fingerpicking attack	5kHz–7kHz	Boost
Acoustic guitar	Less low-end mud	60Hz–80Hz	Cut
	More body/warmth	200Hz–250Hz	Boost
	More pick attack	3kHz–7kHz	Boost
Conga	Less boom	50Hz–60Hz	Cut
	More attack hand on skin	3kHz–7kHz	Boost
Shaker	Less room noise	100Hz and below	Cut and roll off
	More clarity	2kHz–3kHz	Boost
Clave	Less room noise	100Hz and below	Cut and roll off
	More wood attack	2kHz–5kHz	Boost
Vocal	More low-end presence	60Hz–80Hz	Boost
	Less nasal quality	300Hz–400Hz	Cut
	S's too overpowering	3kHz–5kHz	Cut
	More *S*'s for diction	3kHz–5kHz	Boost
	More brilliance/air	10kHz–12kHz	Boost

More Recording Tips

Scheduling Tracking & Mixing Sessions

In order to save time, money, and gas, as well as to appease impatience, many local bands want to mix immediately after tracking. Do everything possible to dissuade them from doing this. Most people don't realize it, but listening to music, especially listening intently, can tire the ears (and mind). This is true even at moderate volume levels. After a day of tracking, nobody will be able to hear as accurately or think as clearly. Mixing should start with fresh ears and minds. Make this clear when booking time for a client and stress the fact that it will not actually cost any more, as it is the same number of hours. The mixing process may even take fewer hours, since everyone is fresh and there is less chance of having to do things over.

Digital Gain Structures

One of the most common mistakes in the 24-bit digital studio is tracking or mixing with too much gain. Since 0dB is the maximum, anything over this level will clip and distort. Don't do it! (Except maybe as an intentional special effect.)

Most people who understand and follow the 0dB guideline, however, still use too much gain. When tracks are recorded at –6dB, they each have 6dB of headroom before clipping. When 24 such tracks are mixed to stereo, however, they can sum to much greater. On average, in fact, they sum to around 14dB greater when all are active. That –6dB per track now becomes +8 or even more! The clipping will be severe.

In the 24-bit world, a peak tracking level of –24 is a fine level. There's still much less quantization noise than you would get when using a –12dB reference in 16 bits (if that had you worried).

Do not confuse these guidelines with analog or mic preamp levels of any kind. I am just talking about levels to hard disk.

Final Mixes

When making digital mixes, it is often a good idea to create a few different versions. This gives clients options to consider over the course of the week, and they might come in handy if the band gets signed to a major label and the mastering engineer wants some headroom and options to work with. The following is a list of some suggested options:

1. Final mix "mastered" at –1dB to –.01dB peak.

2. Final mix at –4dB peak.

3. Final mix at –4dB peak, no compression or limiting on the stereo bus.

4. Final mix at –4dB peak, vocals up 3dB.

5. Final mix at –4dB peak, vocals down 3dB.

Chapter Summary

1. Thorough preproduction planning helps bring unity, clarity, and focus to a project and generates a more consistently high level of recordings. This includes meeting with performers to solidify a vision for the work, as well as planning performer and microphone placements.

2. A great acoustic space, even paired with the best mics, does not guarantee a good recording. Modes, reflections, and performance issues can happen anywhere, at any time. A critical ear and precise sonic vision must be paired with careful mic placement, acoustical manipulations, and EQ-ing techniques to make the best of any situation.

3. Tracking with EQ can be a time-saving technique that helps to inspire the performers. With a little practice, you can use a good parametric EQ to solve noise, interference, and tonal quality problems quickly and easily.

4. Since digital levels only go up to 0dB, and multitracking requires a significant amount of headroom for bussing, tracking levels should be kept to around –24dB peak. In 24 bits, this level still offers a significant improvement in the signal-to-noise ratio over 16-bit recording.

5. Learning to understand and translate subjective terminology into specific technical and artistic tasks is very important when working with clients in any genre.

15. Employees

After reading this chapter, you should be able to:
- Determine what your studio requires in terms of staffing.
- Develop an effective hiring process that includes creating a job description, advertising, and interviewing potential employees.
- Understand the various laws that affect the hiring and employment process.
- Create an effective employment and benefit package to encourage and retain the most qualified candidates.

As your recording studio grows, there will come a point at which you decide to hire more people. This is an important step for any recording studio to take. It takes time to find and train the right employees, and the paperwork involved—including payroll, payroll tax, insurance, etc.—will take you away from actually recording music. However, choosing the right employees can strengthen your studio, providing new ideas and direction and helping your business grow.

Before you embark on the hiring process you should consider your goals for the studio. If you are happy with the amount and type of work you are doing, you may not need to hire extra staff. If you want to expand and even try to franchise your success, you may need a bigger workforce.

The first step in the hiring process is to understand the needs of your recording studio. Look at the various tasks that your studio must accomplish to run at peak efficiency. Creating a formal organization chart helps you look at your studio from a manager's perspective. This chart shows the various positions within the company with lines of connection between these positions for authority, communication, and responsibility. Most large recording studios are divided into three broad divisions: operations, marketing, and finance. Each area includes upper, middle, lower, and frontline management.

The Hiring Process

Once you have created your organizational chart, you're ready to search for and hire someone to perform each task. There are several steps in this process, including: creating a job analysis, writing a job description and announcement, screening applications, and checking references.

Job Analysis

A job analysis is the process of collecting facts about a position and the type of person required to fulfill the tasks involved in that position. Use the form supplied in the appendix, which covers the following categories.

- Job responsibilities. What do you expect the person to do? Include both major responsibilities and day-to-day tasks.

- Education and experience required. What background are you looking for in a candidate? Is having a graduate degree important? Does experience outweigh education?

- Additional skills. Does this person need specialized recording, computer, or marketing skills?

- Supervision. Who will be supervising this employee's work?

Job Description

Now that you've created your job analysis, you should be able to write a job description. This not only clearly defines how a job fits within your studio, but it forms the basis of a classified ad. Use the worksheet in the appendix.

Apart from education, experience, and skills, your job description should include duties and the amount of time (represented as a percentage) the employee will spend in these duties. Also write a brief statement describing your studio.

Writing the Advertisement

Using your job analysis and job description, you can now create an employment advertisement. A good ad, placed in the right media, is crucial for obtaining the best-qualified candidate. An effective ad is written is a manner that shows potential employees that your studio is professional and requires candidates that meet your high standards. To keep your costs down, describe the position in a concise and descriptive manner. Remember, your ad should be accurate and avoid any terms that may imply discrimination (discussed later in this chapter).

All ads should contain the following information:

- Position title. A clear, descriptive title gives the reader an immediate understanding of the position. This should be placed at the head of the ad, in bold or capital letters.

- Position duties. Include the main duties and, if space and cost permit, some of the additional duties that you wish the candidate to complete.

- Experience and education requirements. Clearly state what candidates need in the level and type of education (e.g., bachelor of music required) and the amount of experience (e.g., five years' experience in music production and recording). Specific requirements will discourage unqualified candidates and save you time during the interviewing process. Some ads use terms such as "considered" to open the potential pool of candidates. For example, you might say, "Experience required, undergraduate degree preferred."

- Benefits. List benefits such as overtime, dental, health coverage, etc. To save space and money, you can list only benefits that are especially attractive, such as "Excellent health and dental plans."

- How to respond. You may require a résumé, letters of reference, and proof of qualification (university transcripts). Note how you want these sent, by mail (include your full mailing address), fax (supply the fax number and name of the person to whom they should direct the fax), or e-mail (give details on sending attachments). If the candidate must call for an appointment, give the address, phone number, and contact person. Give clear deadlines for applications. State if you will only consider applications received or sent by a certain date (for example, "Applications accepted until January 1," or "Applications must be postmarked by January 1").

- Attractive features. List some of the features and benefits of working at your studio. This includes working with rock stars, working in the music industry, flexible hours, high pay, etc.

Where to Search

There are many methods of finding employees for your recording studio. Some methods are obvious, like placing a classified ad; others are less so.

- *Classified ads:* You can place classified ads in your local newspaper as well as specialized papers and trade journals. For positions with more general requirements, use the Sunday classifieds.

- *Private employment agencies and search firms:* These agencies usually require a fee for their services. Make sure you find out what screening, interviewing, and testing methods an agency uses. In some cases the fee charged is worth the time and effort you save in the hiring process.

- *Government agencies:* State and local employment services may offer screening, training, and testing services. There may also be financial and tax incentives for using government agencies.

- *Professional organizations:* Many trade organizations have job banks for their members. These are directed toward people interested in your field, even those outside your immediate location. Some organizations publish this information in a newsletter or online.

- *Schools:* Secondary schools, trade schools, community colleges, and universities are a valuable source of potential employees. Many colleges have areas of specialization that may be useful to your studio. Some universities require their students to undertake internships, which give students practical experience and allow employers to receive services for a low fee or for free. You can obtain information on these programs through career services, placement services, or counselors. Knowing high school and college teachers will help direct you to talented students.

- *Internet:* If you have your own Web site, you can create a page that details available positions. Although this is a very inexpensive way of listing a job position, it may attract unqualified employees.

- *Networking:* Most jobs are filled via networking through friends, neighbors, customers, and colleagues. Since your network includes people in the recording industry, it can help you find qualified applicants who come with a ready reference. Networking can also help cut the cost of advertising.

- *Help-wanted signs:* Placing fliers in local businesses is inexpensive but may not be an effective way to find qualified candidates. Furthermore, you may need to spend extra time screening each person.

- *Family:* Your extended family can help solve your staffing needs quickly and inexpensively. It can be risky to mix your business and personal life, though, and firing an employee is easier if you don't share family ties.

Interviewing

Interviewing a pool of candidates is the best method to find a suitable employee. At the interview, you are able to assess the qualifications, communication skills, and values of a potential employee. It is also an opportunity for candidates to learn about the company's structure, goals, and products.

Before actually meeting any candidates, review the applications and select up to four leading candidates. This allows you to interview all the employees in one day. Interviewing is a skill that takes time and preparation to develop. Before your interviews, prepare a list of questions for the applicants. Rank your questions in order of most important for the studio to least important. You might look for the following skills:

- Technical knowledge, as well as a willingness to learn.

- Communication skills, including written, verbal, and listening.

- Leadership and motivation.

- Body language. This is an indication of a person's confidence, maturity, and general positive attitude.

Your questions should not repeat facts covered by the candidate's résumé and application. Questions should concern areas such as education, experience, skills, and goals. They should highlight a candidate's attitudes and personality as well as problem-solving skills.

There are several laws that affect the interviewing of candidates. The Civil Rights Act of 1964 barred discrimination on the basis of race, sex, religion, and national origin in all human resource activities, including hiring, training, promoting, pay, and benefits. This act later became the basis of the Equal Employment Opportunity Commission. The EEOC is a federal agency that enforces federal and state hiring laws and offers guidelines on how to interview applicants. You are not permitted to ask questions that refer to an applicant's:

- Sex, race, creed, or national origin.
- Age. You can only ask questions that satisfy applicable age laws.
- Disabilities. This includes questions on a candidate's psychological state.
- Marital status.
- Criminal record.
- Medical history.
  Here is a list of typical questions you might ask a prospective employee:
- What is your greatest strength/weakness?
- What personality traits do you most admire in another person?
- What personality traits do you least like in another person?
- What did you like about your last job? (Assuming there was a last job.)
- What did you like least about your last job?
- Where do you see yourself in five years?
- What interests you most about this recording studio?

During the interview listen carefully to the candidate's answers. Jot down any answers that impressed or concerned you. You can develop a checklist to rate and compare the candidates. At the conclusion of the interview, leave time for the candidate to ask questions. Be prepared to answer questions regarding work hours, benefits, expectations, company goals, current projects, etc. This is also a chance to see if the candidate has done some homework on your studio. After the interview give yourself time to write down some notes about the candidate, listing their best qualities as well as their skills and knowledge. Keeping consistent notes and questions will aid you in interviewing more than one candidate or preparing you if a second interview is required.

Here is a list of ten factors that you should consider before hiring someone.

1. Communication skills. Does the candidate possess written, verbal, and especially interpersonal skills? Will he or she fit within the culture of the recording studio?

2. Analytical and problem-solving skills. Will the candidate be trainable, learn new skills, and solve problems as they occur?

3. Initiative and drive. Does the candidate have leadership skills? Will he/she set goals for him/herself and the company?

4. Work ethic. Did the candidate show evidence of hard work? Can he/she balance a personal and professional life?

5. Organization skills and time management. Did the candidate provide examples of meeting deadlines, paying attention to details, and producing well-organized work?

6. Enthusiasm and passion. Did the candidate show a positive attitude during the interview? Is he/she passionate enough about the job to remain with it for a period of time?

7. Cooperation. Will the candidate work well with others, especially with you?

8. Technical skills. Does the candidate have the knowledge and skills needed for the position?

9. Leadership skills. Will this candidate lead other members of the studio without supervision? Will he/she inspire respect and trust in others, without being authoritarian?

10. Professionalism. Where you impressed by the candidate's manner, and would he/she exhibit the same professionalism to your customers?

If your candidate falls short in too many of these areas, you may need to ask yourself one more question: Could I find a better candidate? If the answer is yes, you may need to extend the job search.

Checking References

Before hiring someone it is a very good idea to check his or her references. This will often show flaws in a candidate that you could not foresee during an interview and save you the cost of hiring a negligent employee. If you do check references, try to avoid personal recommendations, since they are almost always favorable. The best person who will give an unbiased view of a candidate is a former supervisor. Human resource departments are instructed to offer only a candidate's name, dates of employment, and job title. What you are looking for is someone to give an opinion about the candidate. Here are some questions you might ask a supervisor.

1. How did the person interact with his/her colleagues, supervisors, customers, etc.?

2. How would you describe the candidate's quality of work?

3. Did the candidate have a good attendance record?

4. Why did the candidate leave your company?

5. Would you rehire this candidate?

It is always wise to check as many facts about a candidate before making a decision. Check the candidate's university to obtain degree titles and the dates the candidate attended. If the position requires driving, it is a good idea to check the candidate's record with the motor vehicle registry.

Making Your Choice

Once you have selected an employee and he or she has accepted your offer, you should call or write the other candidates and thank them for their time and effort. If in the future your studio expands you could contact these people to see if they would be interested in a job. It is also very important that you keep the applications and notes of each candidate on file.

For candidates not hired, federal law requires you to keep applications and résumés on file for at least one year. You must keep the application of the person hired for at least three years. This file will form the basis of the new employee's personnel file.

New employees should be taken through an orientation process to help them get off to a good start in their work. Orientation might include introducing them to their colleagues, training them on specialized equipment, and taking them to lunch.

Benefits

Many companies provide benefits in addition to wages as a way to recruit and retain highly qualified employees. Federal and state laws require that companies provide certain benefits. (Employment laws are discussed later in this chapter.) It is important that you clearly set out what benefits you offer and how to apply for them, including any necessary documentation, such as a physician's statement. This reduces the confusion in employees' minds and also helps to prevent legal action against a company if an employee feels that he or she has been unfairly treated. This section deals with common benefits including vacation and sick leave, health insurance, and child care. Other benefits, such as retirement and pension plans, are discussed in the next chapter.

Paid Leave

Many companies offer paid time off as part of their benefits package. Paid leave is not mandated by the government, except in the case of government departments and companies that have union contracts.

Vacation leave is often based on the amount of time contributed and the position a person holds. Many companies offer vacation days after an employee accrues a certain number of working hours. Some companies offer personal days, which are often tied to sick days not used, and flexible summer work schedules when the workload may be reduced.

Most companies are closed for major holidays, such as New Year's Day, President's Day, Memorial Day, Fourth of July, Labor Day, and Thanksgiving. On these days, employees receive full wages. Some companies also offer paid holidays on certain religious holidays, including Good Friday, Christmas Eve, Rosh Hashanah, Yom Kippur, or the Chinese New Year. Other leave-based benefits include leave for funerals, jury duty, voting, and military reserve. It is important that you list any blackout dates when employees are needed in the studio.

Sick leave is often given at a rate similar to that of vacation leave. Many companies grant sick leave to employees each year. If an employee is absent for an excessive period of time, the company may end further sick leave payments. Be aware, though, that any action that seems unfair or discriminatory could lead to legal action against the studio.

Health Insurance

Health insurance is one the most important and expensive benefits offered to employees. Many companies offer generous health and dental insurance to lure the best candidates.

However, the steadily rising costs of health insurance have forced many small businesses to reduce the amount of medical coverage given or to come up with other cost-effective systems. The most common health insurance plans are:

- Managed care. This system includes health maintenance organizations (HMOs), which require employees to use doctors and hospitals that are contracted to the HMO; and preferred provider organizations (PPOs), which allows employees to choose physicians inside or outside the network. In both cases the employee pays a preset amount per office visit, and the insurance pays the remaining amount.

- Traditional indemnity plans. An indemnity plan allows employees to select their own medical providers. Insurance companies reimburse the employee or provider directly.

- Archer Medical Savings Accounts. A studio with 50 or fewer employees can set up an Archer MSA. This system works in conjunction with an insurance policy and the employee's pretax dollars.

Legal Issues

When you hire someone your studio may be subject to several state and federal laws. These govern such issues as wages, dismissal, child labor, discrimination, medical leave, and sexual harassment.

Wages
The Fair Labor Standards Act (FLSA) sets the minimum wage, provides rules for overtime pay, and deals with labor violations, such as child labor. This information must be clearly displayed in the work environment. Overtime is considered any work over 40 hours and must be paid at one and half times the base rate.

A significant amendment to the FLSA was the Equal Pay Act. This law prohibits sexual discrimination in pay, employee benefits, and pensions. It also does not allow employers to lower the wages of either men or women to comply with the law. Any differences in pay and benefits should be based only on seniority, merit, and the quantity and quality of production.

Dismissal
The rules associated with firing an employee vary from state to state. In many states, dismissal is determined by the doctrine of "employment at will," which allows employers to fire employees for any legitimate reason, including breach of contract, either expressed or implied, violation of laws, and violation of public policy. Employees are protected against wrongful termination if the employer fires them based on discrimination, forming or being part of a union, filing a workers' compensation form, reporting employer illegal activities (whistle blowing), refusing to work under unsafe conditions, and jury duty. Many unions protect members from unfair and illegal dismissal.

Child Labor

Laws in the U.S. prohibit the exploitation of minors. Most legislation restricts the type of work a minor can participate in, and the days and number of hours a minor can work.

Discrimination

Discrimination is the denial of opportunities to individuals based on characteristics that have no bearing on their performance. You cannot discriminate against a person based on their race, religion, sexual preference, political affiliation, national origin, marital status, or age. If your studio has more than 15 employees you are subject to numerous federal laws. When hiring staff you need to make sure that your decisions are solely based on education, experience, and skills related to specific job duties.

Exemption from these law does occur in some cases: when hiring on native lands; when religious organizations are hiring people for specific religious tasks; and where a person's sex or national origin are job qualifications (e.g., a female vocalist is needed for a jingle).

Medical Leave

The Pregnancy Act of 1978 prohibits discrimination in the hiring, promotion, or termination of women because they are pregnant. It is also illegal to force an employee to resign or take a leave of absence because of pregnancy. Maternity leave is based on the employee's ability to work, and an employer must treat pregnancy like any other temporary health condition. These laws were updated and expanded in the 1993 Family and Medical Leave Act (FMLA), which grants employees 12 weeks of unpaid leave for adoption and serious medical conditions of a spouse, child, or parent. Most states have legislation that complies with the FMLA or surpasses it.

Sexual Harassment

Sexual harassment is defined as any unwelcome advances or conduct that creates an intimidating, hostile, or offensive work environment. It is a serious problem that can affect any type or size of company. There are two forms of sexual harassment: quid pro quo (this for that) and hostile work environment harassment.

Quid-pro-quo harassment is defined as making promotion, pay increases, employment, or benefits contingent upon sexual demands. A hostile working environment is one in which sexual behavior makes the work environment intimidating or hostile. This could include offensive language or display of sexual material. The best way for a studio to prevent sexual harassment is to have a strict written policy in this matter. Employers should also act immediately on any complaints, often to an impartial third party who can investigate the claim and recommend action. Your regional EEOC or state Fair Employment Practices offices can refer you to independent agencies that carry out such work.

These other labor laws and agencies may be important to your recording studio:

* The Americans with Disabilities Act (ADA) prohibits the discrimination against individuals with physical or mental handicap in hiring, promotion, and compensation.

This law requires companies to make reasonable accommodations for such employees, ranging from special ramps for access to parking facilities set aside for employees with disabilities.

- The Occupational Safety and Health Administration (OSHA) was established to reduce occupational injury and illness. OSHA requires all companies to have a safe working environment by providing adequate ventilation, exits, and protective equipment. OSHA can inspect facilities without warning.

- The National Labor Relations Act (Wagner Act) and the Taft-Hartley Act gives employees the right to start a union and be a member of a union.

Alternatives to Full-Time Employment

The employment of full-time staff can be expensive for small start-up recording studios. Alternative forms of employment can offer advantages to the studio, including reduced costs in wages and benefits.

Temporary Employees
Many employment agencies offer temporary workers for a short-term basis. You can hire these workers at times when the regular staff is on holiday or leave, or during periods of extra work. Another advantage of temporary workers is that the employment agency often pays for medical benefits, vacation pay, and other benefits. One of the biggest drawbacks associated with temporary workers, however, is the time required for training. Temporary workers are best used to fill in roles that require little or no training.

Part-Time Employees
Part-time employees solve many of the problems associated with temporary workers. Since part-timers are in many respects permanent employees, the time and effort associated with training these staff members pays off in the longer term. Like temporary workers, part-time employees are not offered health insurance, paid vacation, or retirement benefits.

Job Sharing
Job sharing is similar to part-time employment, but in this case two people share the duties and requirements of a full-time position. The advantage for a recording studio is that two people can easily handle the workload of one employee and can, in fact, end up doing the work of two or more full-time workers. On the other hand, job sharing requires that employees are managed very well in their job duties. The additional administration and costs of payroll tax, insurance, and benefits may make the job-sharing position more expensive than using a full-time employee.

Consultants
Consultants are a viable alternative if you wish to hire someone for a specific task. The advantage of consultants is that they have specialized training. For example, your studio may use an

independent producer for a particular recording or a tax consultant to handle the studio's tax and accounting issues. The added advantage is that you pay no taxes for a consultant.

Interns

Many colleges and universities have music business and/or sound recording technology programs. These institutions' degree programs often require their students to undertake internships. In many cases students will work for free or a small amount of money in exchange for class credit and the ability to earn working experience.

A disadvantage of using interns is that you must plan an effective work schedule for them and spend time monitoring their performance. However, the advantages often outweigh the disadvantages, as having free, talented students with specialized training and skills may offset the lack of experience. Furthermore, you may eventually hire the intern, without the need to go through the expense of a job search.

Outsourcing

Outsourcing is an important function for many companies today. Many recording studios offer clients specialized services completed by outside companies. These range from graphic design for album covers to the manufacturing and distribution of CDs. When using outsourcers, be sure to check the references of the companies as well as the quality of their work and their ability to meet the deadlines you impose. Remember, if they do not meet your standards and requirements, your recording studio will end up with the bad reputation or lose hard-earned customers.

Chapter Summary

1. The hiring process involves five steps: writing a job analysis, writing a job description, creating an ad using the most appropriate media, screening potential candidates via an interview process, and making a decision that best suits your studio's needs.

2. Hiring laws are strictly enforced to protect the rights of a candidate against discrimination. You should be aware of laws that prohibit a company from basing a hiring decision on sex, race, marital status, age, or medical history.

3. Benefits help attract the best-qualified candidate to your studio. Some common benefits include health insurance, vacation pay, sick leave, maternity leave, and retirement plans.

4. There are several federal and state laws that protect employees' rights, including the Fair Labor Standards Act, the Americans with Disabilities Act, and the Family and Medical Leave Act. Many of these laws are administered by the Equal Employment Opportunity Commission and the Occupational Safety and Health Administration, which monitor businesses' compliance with laws on sexual harassment, job safety, child labor, and discrimination.

5. Many alternatives to full-time employment exist today. Part-time employees, temporary employees, and outsourcing can reduce the costs associated with full-time staff.

16. Employee Taxes & Retirement Plans

After reading this chapter, you should be able to:
- **Understand employee taxes.**
- **Be aware of the rules concerning Social Security and Medicare tax.**
- **Offer employees a range of retirement plans.**

A major component of tax collection is associated with employees. If your recording studio has employees, you must pay various federal and state income taxes, Social Security, unemployment, and Medicare taxes. These taxes may be due at different times of the financial year and require the studio owner to withhold certain amounts from employees. To further complicate the situation, a studio owner is responsible for filing taxes at the appropriate time. If you do not comply with IRS regulations you may be fined or even forced to close. It is recommended that you consult a knowledgeable accountant about tax matters.

Before we can discuss employee taxation, we must define the difference between an employee and a contractor. If your studio controls the means by which a person does a task, then that person can be considered an employee. If the studio only controls the results, a worker is considered an independent contractor. This is important in dealing with payroll taxes, tax withholding, and other bookkeeping duties. The IRS has a complex system of determining whether an employee fits under this category or not. For example, someone hired to file your taxes may be considered an independent contractor, since he sets his own hours, does not need training from the studio owner, and cannot be fired by the studio owner as long as he completes the tasks set forth in a contract.

For your employees, you must complete a W-4. This form indicates your employees' tax status and the withholding amount. Companies must use the government formula to determine income withholding amounts on each paycheck at the rate of 15 percent, 28 percent, 31 percent, and 36 percent. This amount is paid quarterly to the government, though in some states (such as New Hampshire) there is no withholding. A W-4 also requires your studio to file an EIN number (see chapter 13). Once the paperwork is completed you must pay a series of taxes for yourself and your employees.

As an employer you may be responsible for Social Security and Medicare tax. Collectively they are legislated by the Federal Insurance Contribution Act (FICA). The current rate is 7.65 percent for employees, based on their gross wages. As an employer you must pay a matching amount of FICA taxes for each employee. If you are self-employed, you need to pay self-employment tax, at the rate of 15.3 percent. Payment is due each quarter, unless you have over $5,000 of tax, in which case you file for the fiscal year. The maximum amount of self-employment income subject to Social Security tax is $87,900.

Social Security tax is broken down into two categories:

- OASDI (Old Age, Survivors, and Disability Insurance) is 6.2 percent for the first $65,400 in wages.

- HI (Hospital Insurance), which is 1.45 percent on all income.

Collected quarterly, FUTA (Federal Unemployment Tax Act) is used after an employee has been laid off. You need to pay FUTA if your studio meets two criteria: you pay over $1,500 in employee wages, and you have at least one employee working more than 20 hours per week. The current FUTA rate is 6.25 percent for the first $7,000. Some states require you to file a report listing your tax liability.

In many cases your business structure determines what you need to pay in taxes. Sole proprietors do not pay unemployment taxes for themselves. However, a sole proprietorship may be required to provide retirement plans for employees. In the case of a partnership, each partner must include a statement of the partnership's distribution, income, losses, deductions, and/or credits on his or her federal income tax (form 1040). Since the partner's cash income is not a salary, there is no tax withholding at the source and each partner must pay self-employment taxes as if he or she were a sole proprietor. Since no income tax is withheld, partners must make estimated payments quarterly for federal and state purposes. Like sole proprietorships, partnerships do not pay unemployment tax. Finally, corporations pay federal insurance, Social Security, and unemployment taxes.

W-2 forms (wage and tax statements) are due for each employee at the end of January, and the federal copy is due at the IRS on February 28. This form indicates what an employee earned and the amount of federal and state taxes that have been deducted.

Retirement Plans

Retirement plans are essential for employees and employers alike. They prepare employers and employees for a stable income at retirement. There are five types of retirement plans: individual retirement account (IRA), Roth IRA, 401(k), Keogh, and SEP plans.

Individual Retirement Account

This tax-qualified retirement plan is available for employees and employers. The amount is tax deferred, until you withdraw the funds. The total amount you can contribute is $3,000 per year, and you can only use this system if you don't participate in an employer-sponsored retirement plan. As a business owner, you can establish a SIMPLE IRA plan if you have fewer than 100 staff members who receive over $5,000. An employer must make a 3 percent contribution for each employee or a 2 percent contribution for all employees. As of 2005, employees can contribute up to $10,000 annually to a SIMPLE IRA.

Roth IRA

Although Roth IRAs are not tax deductible, the amount you withdraw at retirement is not taxed. You can contribute $3,000 per year as long as you're not participating in an employer-sponsored retirement plan, such as a 401(k). Furthermore, you can only use a Roth IRA if your gross income is less than $95,000 for a single person and $150,000 for a married couple.

401(k)

There are several types of 401(k) plans available for recording studio owners. A standard 401(k) plan allows an employee to defer a percentage of his or her salary, tax-free until distributed at retirement. This plan has several advantages over an IRA. The amount you can contribute is greater, currently $12,000 ($15,000 by 2006), plus it allows the employee to have multiple retirement plans and there is some flexibility in the withdrawal of money before the retirement date (usually there is a fine of 10 percent for withdrawals before the age of 59½.) One problem that many companies come across with 401(k) plans is that the IRS needs to test the plan to ensure that it does not discriminate against higher paid employees. The testing method may be complicated and time consuming. Many companies avoid this by adopting pre-approved 401(k) plans. Information on these plans is available from the IRS.

A SIMPLE 401(k) retirement plan is very similar to a SIMPLE IRA. This new plan is only available for a small business of 100 or fewer employees that doesn't offer any other retirement plan. An employee can contribute up to $10,000 per year (as of 2005) to this plan tax-free. With this system you must either match your employees' contributions up to 3 percent of their gross wages, or contribute a nonelective amount of 2 percent for every employee.

Keogh Plan

The Keogh or HR10 plan is designed for self-employed business owners. The maximum you can contribute to a Keogh plan is determined by the amount that you earn. As with 401(k) plans, withdrawals cannot be made before the age of 59½ or the contributor will face penalties.

Simplified Employee Pension

The SEP plan is the simplest retirement plan available. The plan is suitable for any sized business, even for a self-employed studio owner. Employees do not contribute to SEPs. An employer's contribution is based on a percentage of the employee's earnings or wages. The maximum amount an employer contributes to a SEP is 25 percent of an employee's compensation or $40,000, whichever is less. Contributions are not required every year.

Chapter Summary

1. To complete payment on employee's taxes a recording studio owner needs to complete a W-4 form, determine the income withholding amount, and supply an employer identification number (EIN).

2. Employers are responsible for filing and contributing to several employment taxes, including: the Federal Insurance Contribution Act (FICA); the Federal Unemployment Tax Act (FUTA); Old Age, Survivors, and Disability Insurance (OASDI); and Hospital Insurance (HI).

3. Retirement plans are an important benefit and a way to attract qualified employees. There are four types of retirement plans: IRA, 401(k), Keogh, and SEP.

17. Expanding the Business

After reading this chapter, you should be able to:
- Determine if expansion is right for you.
- Make choices regarding how to approach expansion.
- Prepare a plan for how to increase your market.

here are three main reasons to make major changes to your studio:

1. You're doing great and need to change to keep up with the potential.

2. You're doing fine, but the gear or spaces are getting old and must be replaced.

3. You're doing poorly to OK and see the opportunity to make a positive change.

All three of these can be reasonable cause for change. This short chapter is intended to give guidance on what and when to change—and if you should expand at all. Before going ahead with any major expansion, prove to yourself in a logical and thorough manner that it is a wise idea.

Upgrading Studio Status

If you have been diligent, intelligent, creative, and lucky enough to do well in your studio business and are now considering expansion or upgrade, congratulations! As you are probably aware, small businesses fail much more often then not, so you must be doing something right. For the purposes of this chapter, we'll assume you are looking to do something major, such as changing the location or space of the studio, changing recording platforms, completely overhauling the studio's acoustics, or adding personnel. Before going ahead with any major studio upgrades, be aware: The changes can be painful, or deadly, if not done quickly and with great care.

First, there's the possible downtime. In the recording business, if you are not available to do one gig, you may not get another chance. Be sure to let every one of your clients know exactly what is going to happen and when they should expect you to be back in action. Give them a couple of months' notice so they can get in early if they've got an important project. Offer them incentives to record within a certain amount of time after the upgrade is complete. If you can reel them back in right away, you just may keep them as clients. As for new potential clients, keep the phones manned and offer incentives for waiting as well. Most important, make any downtime as short as possible.

Second, there's the matter of Murphy's Law (you know, if something can go wrong, it will). When you're dealing with technology, properties, contractors, and clients, as well as time and financial constraints, the chances of having some unpleasant surprises are pretty good. Be prepared for the project to take a bit longer and cost a bit more than anticipated. Have contingency plans as well as extra capital.

Finally, there's the chance that you are overestimating the need for such an upgrade. Consider the following:

- Is there a market demand for it?

- Will you lose business if you don't upgrade?

- Is there an audio or technological need for it?

- Are the costs of the change reasonable and in line with income projections?

The answers to most or all of these should be "yes" for serious consideration of any expensive upgrades. If your decision is to go ahead, it may be wise to reread previous chapters of this book for any subject matter relating to your current upgrades.

Expanding Clientele

It is not uncommon to realize, after starting a service business, that you either overestimated the demand for your particular specialty or underestimated the demand for another. Quite a number of rock-band studios struggled to make it work until they noticed they were getting more calls for music production, multimedia, or solo hip-hop projects. When they switched their way of thinking and modified their approach to reaching clientele in these new markets, they became much more successful.

Of course it's not always necessary to switch completely over to a new area. Sometimes you can just modify the emphasis of your marketing strategy and advertising. Don't lose out on a greater opportunity by having a closed mind to the possibilities in your area. Just be sure you actually have the equipment, time, expertise, and personnel to do the additional work right.

The list of possible clients and services given back in chapter 2 is a good one to draw from:

- Record labels

- Producers

- Musical groups (any genre)

- Church groups

- School groups
- Solo artists
- Remixers
- Club music composers
- Radio stations
- Large businesses
- Advertising agencies
- Multimedia companies
- Web-design companies
- Books on tape
- Mastering
- Duplication services
- Location recording
- Post-production
- Rehearsal space rental
- Music lessons
- On-hold audio
- Voice-mail systems
- Audio restoration
- Retail sales
- Game development companies

You can find information on these groups through Web sites, phone directories, journals, newspapers, clubs, professional societies, and books.

A short outline of some of the likely areas for expansion is given below. Further discussion can be found in chapter 2.

Multimedia

Multimedia work requires a thorough knowledge of data compression schemes, synthesis engines, and computer programming. Gear would need to involve more synthesis, MIDI, samplers and sample CDs, video sync (in window) capabilities in the DAW software, and wacky effects plug-ins. The emphasis will be on the computer—you'll need a fast CPU with plenty of RAM. File swapping and system/file compatibility are very important.

If multimedia becomes the main studio focus, a midsize booth and control room may be all that's required. In addition, the mic and preamp collection could be downsized considerably.

Clientele could include game developers, ad agencies, Web designers, large church groups, and dedicated multimedia companies.

Voice-overs

Voice-over work is similar to multimedia, but requires even less gear. You need a good library of effects and licensed music CDs, and MIDI production capabilities and skills are a plus. A booth and control room are all that is required.

In order to hook clients, you need to have a list of talent and their audio demos to play for ad executives. Also, be prepared to give quotes on studio time and talent services on the spot.

Possible clients for voice-overs include all those listed under multimedia above, plus radio stations, solo artists, and companies that produce voice-mail systems, on-hold audio, and audio books.

Post-Production

Local videographers, television stations, large businesses, multimedia companies, and ad agencies are all possible sources for this type of work. Post-production requires video gear and synchronization equipment, most likely S-VHS and/or DV-Pro. DAW software must be able to sync to video or on-screen movies. Limited video editing may also be needed. MIDI and synthesis equipment are essential, as is a large collection of sound effects discs and licensed music beds. Commercial online subscriptions to these types of sound files and MIDI files are available for a monthly fee.

18. Looking Ahead

Starting and running a recording studio is a time consuming and difficult undertaking. This book should have you well prepared to survive in the music business. To optimize your long-term success, consider these final thoughts and guidelines.

Improve your products or services

Even if your product or service has helped you to be a leader in the industry, there is always the need to improve. With competition you may need to change and develop aspects of your products. This is all part of the business life cycle.

Invest in your staff

If you have followed carefully the directions given to you in the chapter on employees, you should have a group of people who are well qualified, experienced, and talented. It is your job as the studio owner to consistently improve employee performance. This is achieved in several ways:

- Give your staff the avenue and flexibility to improve the products and services.

- Trust your staff to get the work done. Being a micromanager only builds fear and resentment in people.

- Break down barriers among your staff members. Work as a team to solve problems.

- Give your staff the opportunity to constantly improve their skills through education and training. You can pay for them to take courses and classes at local universities and colleges, or to attend conferences and meetings. This cost will pay off for you in the long term.

Look to growth

It is important that you not stay in one place. Companies that are complacent or static often find that small, flexible competitors end up taking over the market or putting them out of business.

Concentrate on creativity and innovation

Creativity is the cornerstone of the music industry. A successful studio is defined by its creative and innovative approaches.

Constantly plan

Recording studio planning should not end at the start-up stage. Fiscal and structural planning should be part of your long-term development. You can use many of these plans to obtain further capital from banks, financial institutions, and investors.

Learn from failure

Even with the best plans, capital, and talent, your studio may face the surprises and difficulties that occur in the music business. The best method to deal with failure is to learn from past mistakes and factor them into your future plans.

Do what you love

Your recording studio requires a huge commitment of time and effort. No money or fame will ever replace the day-to-day enjoyment of working in a field that you love. Even during the times when the most mundane details of running your studio weigh heavily on you, remember that most people need to work in fields they do not like in order to make a living. We hope you will prosper in a field you love.

Part III
Appendix

Worksheets

Personal Financial Statement

Personal Financial Statement

_____ _____ ,2_____

Assets
Cash   _____
Savings accounts   _____
Stocks, bonds, and other securities   _____
Accounts/notes receivable   _____
Life insurance cash value   _____
Rebates/refunds   _____
Autos/other vehicles   _____
Real estate   _____
Vested pension plan/retirement accounts   _____
Other assets   _____

                              TOTAL ASSETS $ _____

Liabilities
Accounts payable   _____
Taxes   _____
Real estate loans   _____
Other liabilities   _____

                         TOTAL LIABILITIES $ _____

TOTAL ASSETS LESS TOTAL LIABILITIES
NET WORTH $ _____

Monthly Household Cash Needs

Monthly Household Cash Needs

Nonstudio Income

Family income	_____	Debt repayment	_____
Investment income	_____	Auto loans	_____
Other income	_____	Credit card debt	_____
Less income taxes	_____	Discretionary expenses	_____
Net monthly income	_____	Entertainment	_____
		Vacation	_____
MONTHLY EXPENSES		Retirement	_____
Housing		Investment savings	_____
Mortgage/rent	_____	Charitable contributions	_____
Utilities	_____	Dues, magazines, etc.	_____
Insurance	_____	Professional fees	_____
Property taxes	_____	**Total Monthly Expenses**	_____
Home repairs	_____		
		Monthly Surplus/Deficit	_____
Living expenses			
Groceries	_____	**Total Year Surplus/Deficit**	
Telephone	_____	(Monthly x 12)	_____
Tuition	_____		
Transportation	_____	**AVAILABILITY TO COVER DEFICIT**	
Medical	_____	Checking accounts	_____
Clothing	_____	Savings accounts	_____
Personal	_____	Money market accounts	_____
		Personal credit lines	_____
Insurance Premiums		Marketable securities	_____
Auto insurance	_____	**TOTAL ASSETS**	_____
Medical insurance	_____		
		NEEDED RESERVES	
		Total assets–deficits	_____

Assets

```
                              Assets


                        (Figures shown in $)
                                        September 30, 2_____
                                        2 _____        2 _____
Current Assets
Cash                                    _____        _____
Funds                                   _____        _____
Local bank account                      _____        _____
Operating account                       _____        _____
Petty cash account                      _____        _____
Savings account                         _____        _____
Credit cards                            _____        _____
              Current Assets Total      _____        _____
Accounts Receivable
City ledger                             _____        _____
Employees                               _____        _____
Other                                   _____        _____
Federal income tax refund               _____        _____
          Accounts Receivable Total     _____        _____
Inventory
(Paid studio equipment and supplies)    _____        _____
                   Inventory Total      _____        _____

Prepaid Expenses
Insurance                               _____        _____
Other                                   _____        _____
            Prepaid Expenses Total      _____        _____


                   TOTAL ASSETS         _____        _____
```

Estimating Start-up Costs

Estimating Start-up Costs

ITEM	AMOUNT
Fixtures and equipment	$ _____
Store and/or office supplies	$ _____
Remodeling and decorating	$ _____
Deposits on utilities	$ _____
Insurance	$ _____
Installation of fixtures	$ _____
Legal fees	$ _____
Telephone	$ _____
Rental	$ _____
Licenses and permits	$ _____
Advertising and promotion	$ _____
Sound recording equipment	$ _____
Total Estimated Start-up Cost	$ _____

Heat, Light & Power Expenses

Heat, Light & Power Expenses

(Figures shown in $)

Expenses	Year ended September 30 20 _____	20 _____
Electricity	_____	_____
Electric bulbs and supplies	_____	_____
Fuel—gas	_____	_____
Water	_____	_____
Waste removal	_____	_____
Total heat, light, and power expenses	_____	_____

Repairs & Maintenance

Repairs & Maintenance

(Figures shown in $)

Year ended September 30

20 _____ | 20 _____

Expenses
Building
Electrical and mechanical equipment
Sound recording equipment
Furniture and furnishings
Painting and decorating
Heating and air-conditioning
Engineering supplies
Labor costs

Total repairs and maintenance expenses

Advertising Worksheet

Advertising Worksheet

Form of Advertising	Size of audience	Frequency of use	Cost of a single ad	Estimated cost
		×	= $
		×	= $
		×	= $
		×	= $
		×	= $
		×	= $
		×	= $
		×	= $

Total = $_____

Liability & Owner's Equity

Liability & Owner's Equity

(Figures shown in $)

Year ended September 30, 2 _____

Current Liabilities
Note payable   _____

Accounts Payable
Trade   _____
Other   _____

Taxes Payable and Accrued
Federal income taxes   _____
Payroll   _____
Sales and occupancy   _____
Real estate and personal property   _____

Accrued Expenses
Salaries and wages   _____
Management fee   _____
Utilities   _____
Other   _____

Total Current Liabilities   _____
Long-Term Debt   _____
Owner's Equity   _____

Income Statement

Income Statement

Year ended December 31, 2_____

Net Sales _____
Cost of Goods Sold _____

Gross Profit _____

Operating Expenses
Selling expenses _____
General expenses _____
Administrative expenses _____

Total Operating Expenses _____

Income from Operations _____

Other Income
Interest expense (_____)
Interest income _____
Other _____

Total Net Other Income (Expense) _____

Net Income before Taxes _____

Statement of Cash Flow

Statement of Cash Flow

Year ended December 31, 2 _____

Beginning cash balance _____

Cash Receipts
Collections _____
Interest _____
Long-term debt _____
Equity financing _____

Total Receipts _____

Disbursements
Operating expenses _____
Direct labor costs _____
Capital expenditure _____

Total Disbursements _____

Net Cash Flow _____

Net Increase/Decrease in Cash _____

Cash and Cash Equivalents at Beginning of Year _____

Cash and Cash Equivalents at End of Year _____

Balance Sheet

Balance Sheet

Date _____

Assets
  Current Assets
    Cash   _____
    Accounts receivable   _____
  Merchandise inventories   _____
    Total Current Assets   _____

  Fixed Assets
    Land   _____
    Building   _____
    Equipment   _____
    Total Fixed Assets   _____
    Total Assets   1. _____

Liabilities
  Current Liabilities
    Accounts payable   _____
    Note payable   _____
    Payroll taxes payable   _____
    Total Current Liabilities   _____

  Long-term liabilities
    Mortgage payable   _____
    Long-term note   _____
    Total Long-Term Liabilities   _____
    Total Liabilities   2. _____

Owner's Equity
  Proprietor's Capital   3. _____
    Total Liabilities and Owner's Equity   (2 & 3) _____

Job Analysis Form

Job Analysis Form

Position title: _____ Date: _____
Prepared by: _____
Job responsibilities: _____
_____
_____
Education and experience required: _____
_____
_____
Skills: _____
_____
_____
Additional requirements: _____
_____
_____
_____
Department: _____
Supervisor: _____

Job Description

Job Description

Position title: _____ Date: _____
Prepared by: _____
Job summary: _____
_____
_____
Primary duties:
1. _____
2. _____
3. _____
4. _____
5. _____

Additional duties:
1. _____
2. _____
3. _____
4. _____
5. _____

Department: _____
Supervisor: _____

Resources

General Business

American Management Association
An association that provides management and educational services to business professionals.

www.amanet.org

American Marketing Association
A resource for marketing publications, seminars, and other information associated with marketing.

www.marketingpower.com

AnnualReports.com
This Web site lists annual reports and is a valuable tool for comparing your recording studio's report with those of major businesses.

www.annualreports.com

Hoover's
This Web site provides a vast amount of information on over 1,000 companies, including company profiles, financial status, and history.

www.hoovers.com

Service Corps of Retired Executives
SCORE is a national organization of retired business executives that provides free counsel and workshops for small business owners.

www.score.org

USADATA
An excellent site for market research.

www.usadata.com

Government Agencies

Bureau of Economic Analysis
This federal agency evaluates U.S. economic activity. The site offers numerous economics reports.

www.bea.doc.gov

Bureau of Labor Statistics
An important Web resource for comparing businesses is the "Annual Report Gallery."

www.bls.gov

Census Bureau
The Census Bureau provides a wealth of information for market research. Statistics on everything from the U.S. balance of trade to total sales of all U.S. multinational companies in the service sector can be found in this invaluable resource.

www.census.gov

Copyright Office
The Copyright Office handles copyright registrations and provides extensive information and forms online.

www.copyright.gov

Economics & Statistics Administration
This organization provides most of the economic data produced by the federal government.

www.esa.doc.gov

Federal Trade Commission (FTC)
This site offers information on rules and requirements for effective business, as well as on business and trade associations.

www.ftc.gov

Internal Revenue Service (IRS)
The IRS Web site offers information on U.S. tax policy as well as taxation forms.

www.irs.gov

Minority Business Development Agency (MBDA)
The MBDA fosters minority entrepreneurs in the U.S. This site offers information on marketing, finance, law, and government regulation.

www.mbda.gov

Occupational Safety & Health Administration (OSHA)

OSHA's Web site offers information on workers' health and safety regulations.

www.osha.gov

Office of Business Liaison

This office is a link between the business community and the government. It offers information on government legislation and business issues.

www.osec.doc.gov/obl

Patent & Trademark Office

The PTO provides a wealth of information for patent and trademark application. The PTO is also a good source of information on reviews and technological data.

www.uspto.gov

Small Business Administration (SBA)

The SBA offers a wealth of support, information, and counsel. Apart from financial assistance, the SBA presents workshops and seminars and provides professional referrals.

www.sba.gov

Music Industry Organizations

Alliance of Artists & Recording Companies

A nonprofit organization established to distribute both U.S. and international royalties to artists and recording companies.

www.aarcroyalties.com

American Federation of Musicians (AFM)

A labor union representing the interests of musicians in the U.S. and Canada.

www.afm.org

American Federation of Television & Radio Artists (AFTRA)

A labor union representing artists in the entertainment and news industry.

www.aftra.org

American Society of Composers, Authors & Publishers (ASCAP)

A performing rights organization that collects royalties for members from nondramatic public performances.

www.ascap.com

Audio Engineering Society

A professional society devoted to audio technology.

www.aes.org

Broadcasting Music Incorporated (BMI)

A performing rights organization that collects royalties for members from nondramatic public performances.

www.bmi.com

Harry Fox Agency

An organization for the collection and payment of mechanical royalties.

www.harryfox.com

Home Recording Rights Coalition (HRRC)

A lobbying organization for the protection and use of noncommercial recording products.

www.hrrc.org

Music Managers Forum

A forum for the dissemination of information between managers in the music industry.

www.mmfus.com

National Association of Recording Merchandisers (NARM)

A trade group that serves the music retailing community in areas of advocacy, education, and promotion.

www.narm.com

National Music Publishers' Association (NMPA)

An advocacy organization for music publishers, which also houses the Harry Fox Agency.

www.nmpa.org

Recording Industry Association of America (RIAA)

A trade organization for the recording industry.

www.riaa.com

SESAC

A performing rights organization that collects royalties for members from nondramatic public performances.

www.sesac.com

Society of Professional Audio Recording Services (SPARS)

A professional organization for the dissemination of information and education on the subject of recording studio equipment.

www.spars.com

Magazines

Acoustic Guitar

A magazine for acoustic guitarists with interviews, workshops, and reviews.

www.acousticguitar.com

Billboard

Music industry publication.

www.billboard.com

EQ

Recording industry magazine.

www.eqmag.com

Mix

Recording industry magazine.

www.mixonline.com

Recording

Recording industry magazine.

www.recordingmag.com

Studio Equipment & Services

Acoustics First

Acoustics products of all kinds.

www.acousticsfirst.com

Acoustic Sciences Corporation

Acoustics products of all kinds, especially traps.

www.acousticsciences.com

Alactronics

Acoustic design services.

    www.alactronics.com

Apogee

Maker of high-end converters. A great source for the latest technology issues and links.

    www.apogeedigital.com

Auralex Acoustics

Acoustics products of all kinds.

    www.auralex.com

ClearSonic

Drum shields and free-standing sound absorption baffles.

    www.clearsonic.com

Furman Sound

Audio power products.

    www.furmansound.com

Gretch-Ken Industries

Soundproofing products, supplies, and isolation booths.

    www.soundsuckers.com

The Music Center

Sales and support of new music and audio equipment.

    www.musiccenterinc.com

Sweetwater

Sales and support of new music and audio equipment.

    www.sweetwater.com

Whisper Room

Isolation booths.

    www.whisperroom.com

Acoustics Online

Acoustics Forum
forum.studiotips.com

Acoustics, Vibrations & Signal Processing
www.ecgcorp.com

Acoustisoft
www.acoustisoft.com

AudioTester
www.sumuller.de/audiotester

Brown Bear Software
www.brownbear.de

HpW Works
www.hpw-works.com

Metric Halo
www.mhlabs.com/products/

Morset Sound Development
www.nvo.com/winmls/door/

PC AV Tech
www.pcavtech.com

Rhintek
www.rhintek.com

SIA Software Acoustic Tools
www.siasoft.com/products/at.html

Software Resources
staff.niagara.edu/mls/softsor.html

Sound Technology Spectra Series Analysis
www.soundtechnology.com/download-center.htm

TerraSonde
www.terrasonde.com

Recording Practices

Audio Definitions
Glossary of audio terms.

www.nathanspage.com/wftd/wftd-a.html

DigitalAudioGuide.com
Glossary of audio terms.

www.digitalaudioguide.com/glossary.htm

Harmony Central
Music-related ads, articles, and reviews.

www.harmony-central.com

I Write the Music
Recording tips for songwriters.

www.iwritethemusic.com/homerecording.html

ProRec
Resources for the recording professional.

www.prorec.com

Rane Corporation
Pro audio reference.

www.rane.com/digi-dic.html

Recording Hard & Heavy Music

www.powers-court.com/dungeonn.html

World Wide Pro Audio Directory
Links to manufacturers, journals, studios, and professional sites.

www.audiodirectory.nl

Acknowledgments

Creating a book is a collaborative effort. We owe a great debt to the many talented people who helped produce this book, especially Richard Johnston, for believing in this project; Gail Saari, for answering all the endless questions; Jeffrey Pepper Rodgers, for sorting through the mountains of paper to help sculpt this final product; Brad Behling at the Music Center for gallant efforts assembling sample studio setups; and Bernie Mack for sage engineering advice.

Finally, we would like to thank our families and close friends for their support, understanding, and patience during the time spent writing our manuscript. This book would not exist without their help.

About the Authors

John Shirley is an associate professor of music at the University of Massachusetts–Lowell, where he teaches in the sound recording technologies program. He started, and now directs, the university's Contemporary Electronic Ensemble. In addition to his work as a teacher, Dr. Shirley is a recording engineer, studio owner, composer, record producer, software designer, and author. In the summer of 2002, he traveled throughout Cambodia on a Fulbright grant recording traditional Khmer music. He is a contributing editor for *Recording* magazine and has a monthly column entitled "The Compleat Recording Musician." A CD dedicated to Dr. Shirley's original experimental electronic compositions is available on the C74 label (www.cycling74.com/c74/music/009.html). He holds a Ph.D. from the University of Chicago in music composition, with a concentration in computer music.

Richard Strasser is an assistant professor of music industry at Northeastern University, where he teaches music marketing, music entrepreneurship, and performing arts administration. He was formerly executive sales manager at the Stern's Music, a world music label based in London and New York. He is also a performing guitarist and a consultant on music administration issues. Strasser has received numerous awards, including the Queen Elizabeth Silver Jubilee Award, the Australian Arts Council Award, and the Andrés Segovia Award. He serves on the board of directors for the Music and Entertainment Industry Educators Association and the Cultural Organization of Lowell. Strasser holds a DMA in music performance from the Manhattan School of Music.

Index